HOOD LOVER

By
Kasim Power

<u>HOOD LOVER</u>

BLACK P✊WER
Publishing

By
Kasim Power
Author of True Brothers and their pride and joy

Acknowledgements

I welcome you all to my second Novel Hood Lover, and I want to thank God for making this all possible.

First I'd like to thank my editor Shantel Walker for the phenomenal job she did. I'm looking forward to many many projects with you.

Carl Weber thanks for the advice 14 years ago. That advice helped me be able to do what I love doing. Hope Clarke much thanks to you too can't wait for the next project. Zane, Michael Pressley Anthony white, Ho Tep, Ms. Robinson, Domoo, Day Day Jamie thanks for your advice also. To all my people at Moving Mountains let's keep Moving them Mountains. And my people at BlackPowerProduction, Pretty, Odellia, Tracy, Ed, Ronnie, Zali Takaya, Claude, Bobby, Terrance, Lucinie Let's get it. Krystal thanks for being part of this also. To my boy Clive, Komer, Bryon thanks for being part of this project of mine back when I was writing it. Shout out to my boy's Keif, Raymond, Eaton, Clarence, Mo, Bengee, Demoo, Phil, Collie, Mike, Brain, Rudy. Antawn I'm happy for you and your family, and what you doing at Kreative Thinking. Roseland, Bee Bee, Nikki, Lynette thanks for making me work hard on my projects and understanding everything, Also shout out to my cousin Nikki Troy and my big brothers Komer and Ian if it wasn't for me being around you'll back when I was in Junior High school I would have never thought of college and none of this would have happened you guys made sure me and a few others focused on school and life . Ian, Charlie Rock, Sean Hill no matter how many people I dunked on it didn't mean nothing because it wasn't you. I thank you guy because even at the age of 12 I'd be trying to dunk on you'll and get knocked down and you'll would shout now get back up and ball. That's why I was able to do all this because no matter how long it takes I never give up. Qua shout out too you Kima Melina and Selina also my boy Easy Tyrone, D, Kenny,

Will, Josh, Mr. V and then there's the Ladies Marryand, Regina, Latoya, Juli Cotta, Frane you'll keep rising and show that women can succeed and still ho their family's down. Let's get it, Ladies. Earnny, Grace stay watching down c us sisters, Anthony, Kita much love to you. Last but least my family Bella ar Kimora Daddy loves you both. Mom Grandma Uncle Rob and family Cous John, David you'll have a part in this work ethic also. David thanks for puttir up with me in 2002 and teaching me to drive when my own father didn't ha' time too. Aunt Emma and Linda, Shante congratulations to you Larry and K Land Cameron Daylene same to you Madison and Montee. Jasmine Linar Mike, Kevin Asley, Aron, my little brothers I'm proud of you Aunt Debra g well soon Aunt Twala Love you. Pricilla some goes for you too Fatima ar Rose keep doing you're thing I'm proud of your daughters. I have such a hug family and friends and happy that you'll all be part of my life reading ar enjoying Hood Lover. I can be reached BlackPowerProductionPublishing@gmail.com

1
Katrina

It was raining in April 2006 on a Thursday afternoon. Most New Yorkers were enjoying the April showers. I still couldn't seem to erase it from my mind. How could he do this to me after all the things I've done for him? I had just come from a photoshoot in Paris. As I reached for my house keys in my coat pocket, I opened the front door and walked into my apartment. I heard noises, a lot of moaning. I could still picture it.

"What the hell is going on here?" I shouted out. As I entered my bedroom.

"Katrina babe you home early." Darrin was right, I wasn't home until early Monday morning but there was no more talking I immediately started swinging for that Bitch.

Stacy my so-called best friend slept with my fiancée behind my back.

Darrin grabbed my waist because he knew I was ready to go off. "Please, Katrina let me explain. Katrina babe I love you." Wham!! across the face "Motherfucker you expect me to believe that shit. Now I should slap your ass again."

But I quickly paid the price for saying that statement. Next thing I knew I was bleeding from my nose and on the floor.

Darrin stood over me saying… "Now if you will please, let me explain then you'll understand." He paused for a moment and then said … "Stacy and I …I mean what you see now was just a one-night stand. It meant nothing to me and I want you to remember you're the only woman for me."

POW! Stacy punched him in the face saying… "You're lying and you know it.

Darrin, you're the one who was always feeling for me. Telling me how much you want me, how much you need me."

I got back up asking them both how long has this been going on.

"Katrina I don't blame you for being upset with me but it's time you learned the truth. For the past four months, your man has been telling me how much he loves me in bed. Every chance he got and today was different because it happened. From the look on Stacy's face, I knew they did every position including oral Sex. I quickly threw off the Engagement Ring and kicked them both out of my apartment.

Within minutes I went to my parent's house and told them both. My engagement was off. As I explained to my mother what Stacy said to me?

"Sweetie, you must believe in God even though what Stacy did was wrong she should have been able to control her hormones. You must forgive but don't forget. Look at the situation positively. Stacy did you a favor it stopped you from making a huge mistake because if you were married or pregnant with his child you'd be in even more pain."

Now as for Darrin…"

But before my mother could finish I cut her off telling her to forget about Darrin, he's a Dog. "All men are Dogs." Mom all the things

I've done for him, bailing his ass out of jail so many times, and other things. I swear Mom all men are Dogs.

"Excuse me, young lady, you know you're wrong. Now what your mother is trying to say is that your friend was thinking cold-hearted, but we all make mistakes."
"Please, Dad which side are you guys on anyway."
I left their house and I haven't heard from my parents since.
Every message from people who live for me I wouldn't return the call unless it was business.
Six months pass. No one even knew I went back to John Jay Law School to work on my Criminal Law Degree. Being in school again made me feel like a new woman. I still did a little modeling but not nearly as much as before.
As I continued lying in my bed still thinking about the pain I felt that day.
Ring…Ring… I started to pick up my phone but once I saw who it was I decided to just listen.
"Katrina it's me, Stacy, look I'm sorry about what happened back in September. I've been looking for you to tell you to your face how sorry I am. I even went to your Parent's house looking for you one time. Look, girl, we've been best friends since 2nd Grade Let's not let some man come between us. I know you've had tears of pleasure in the past and it was turned into pain because of me. I should have told you a long time ago that your man was flirting with me."
I quickly picked up the phone saying… "You're right Stacy you should be sorry. You fucked my Fiancée when we had just gotten engaged. I want you to know I just dwelled on that emotional pain of what a Dog Darrin turned out to be. But I want you to understand me Bitch I 'm

completely over that. My heart has healed and that pain I suffered on September 14, 2001, I'm leaving it where it belongs in the past."
There was silence on the other end of the phone for a few moments.

"That's good to hear Katrina because I and the girls would like you to come to see the play Lord All Men Can't be Dogs."
I paused for a moment and then told her yes. "Also Stacy I want you to come upstairs before we leave tomorrow night."
As I thought about the answer I had just given her only God knew what was in store for us.

2

Stacy

We all had smiles on our faces because this was something we all looked forward to.

"Girl, can't you drive any faster?" Kalaya said.

"Relax yourself because if you had your license you'd know you have to drive for others, especially in New York City."

I was not about to get into an accident. I had just bought my Toyota Sequoia in February 2002 so I always made sure I drove carefully.

20 minutes later as we reached 5th Ave in Park Slope I started to wonder if I was doing the right thing about inviting Katrina. I mean sure she knew Kalaya and Rose, but I was the reason why we weren't talking in the first place and I felt it was time we made up.

Moments later as I was about to knock on Katrina's door it was already opened. "Welcome back Ms. Bitch!"

"Katrina look I said I was sorry and as I said over the phone we've been best friends too long to let some man come between us."

She just gave me a stare. "Look Katrina things have changed I've changed and after we come from the Beacon Theater we're all going to the Shadow. Look girl you've been hurt I've been hurt 4 times since the last time you've seen me. All I'm saying is it's time we've found our Mr. Do Right."

Within seconds I saw Katrina smile I quickly hugged her and she hugged me back. "Katrina let's both do each other a favor and not let another man come between us."

40 Minutes later we were all in front of the Beacon Theater ready to see the play 'Lord All Men Can't be Dogs.'I told Katrina I was working for Con Edison and how I was able to buy my Toyota Sequoia.

We were all in our seats ready to watch the play

Two hours later when the play was over all four of us brought T-shirts we were all ready to go clubbing. I enjoyed looking at how he could still act.

We were all talking about how we were all going to find a decent man out here in

New York City. Rose on the other hand just didn't give a fuck.

She didn't care if she found a man or not. Rose was one of the Independent sisters out here in New York City.

She had everything going for herself. She was still young in her mid-twenties and had everything a young lady could want a good career at the Post Office her place and about to buy her Ford Expedition.

Kalaya, on the other hand, was the opposite. Every time she had a man she would always lose him to another woman. She would come crying to me always telling me she found out the man was Married or he got back with his Baby Mama.

I used to think Kalaya was crazy for even messing with that kind of man.

That was until I found out the man I was messing with was Married. But would you believe it was his wife who called my house and told me? I was really hurt when she told me that and I could only imagine the pain she was in.

We finally reached the club and I immediately found us a parking spot. Kalaya was the first to get out of the car wearing her short-cut red dress. Her nails were matched lipstick.   "Hurry up ladies it's time to get our drinks on," Kalaya said.

Rose was the second to get out she had on a black suit with heels on.

"Kalaya's Right Stacy You taking long and putting on all that makeup isn't going to get you White as a man but it will get you a one-night stand." Rose said smiling.

As I locked the door to my car I quickly said… "Rose just because you've given up on love doesn't mean we should. Also, I want you to make something clear right now this Sister here stopped those one-night stands a very long time ago." I said trying not to let my ego get the best of me.

"Clam down Girl I was only joking. Look it's time for us to head into this Club let's go have fun." Rose said as all four of us gave each other a high five.

30 Minutes later as we all were in the Shadow I could tell Katrina wasn't too happy about being here. For starters, she was at the Bar drinking and not dancing.

Katrina looked as though she had something on her mind.

I decided to walk up to her. "Katrina, is there something wrong?"

"No, not exactly." She said as she turned to face me.

"It's just that I've thought about what you said earlier. It's time we've found our Mr. Do Right."

'People you don't know how happy I was too here Katrina say that.' I just hugged her. Let's go, Katrina. Let's get our dance on their playing Ginuwine's new song Jeans."

Before we could even reach the dance floor this tall Brother with Dreads walked up to Katrina he quickly touched her hand asking her to dance with him.

As Katrina turned her head I quickly gave her a sign telling her to go dance because the night was still young.

An hour had passed and I went back to the Bar asking the Bartender for a Bacardi light. I was really happy to see Katrina enjoying herself I noticed she was still dancing with that same Brother. 'What a surprise.'

Moments later Kalaya and Rose came to join me at the Bar for a drink.

As I started on my second drink I was explaining to Kalaya and Rose about finding their Mr. Do Right.

"Look, ladies, we've got to believe in God first before he can send us a Mr. Do Right."

Look forget all that bullshit, Stacy, because you of all people should know I don't give a fuck and you'll know I don't mess with a no-cash man."

"I understand that Rose, but sometimes you've got to take a chance."

I quickly explained to both of them about some of these Brothers out here as we all took a view of the Club checking out some of these Brothers in here.

She spotted a man with a nice suit on, but his face was all messed up. You could tell he was one of those Brothers always getting high and he looked like an Alcoholic

"He's probably one of those Niggas who will fuck anything he can. Fuck it he's a Stink Hitter" Rose said.

Rose had a name for all Men. We soon spotted a man in the corner we all could tell he was a Mama's boy no older than 25.

Now Mama Boys are what's up because those are the Men who'll treat you right. They know how to make a Woman happy. The only thing was we couldn't tell if he was mature enough to be a man or if was he still a boy. I quickly turned my head when he saw me looking at him and took another sip of my drink.

"Stacy look out! Because that last guy you were eyeing is headed our way." Kalaya said.

Within seconds he was in my face. "I noticed you were staring at me and I want to tell you straight up you look Sexy."

I quickly crossed my legs as if I didn't want to be bothered.

"Would you like to dance? And by the way, my name is Stephan what's yours?"

I had to admit he even looked better up close, but a sister has to play hard to get.

"You must think you're Mister Valentine, don't you? I'm tired of you men thinking the earth revolves around you."

Clam down Sister all I'm asking is for a dance. Look why don't I buy you and you're girls a drink? I mean I know you had you're drunk already but this one's on me.

Also, I'd like to see you smile. I mean there playing LL Cool J's new song from his 10th Album 'Luv You Better.'

"He's right Girl you need to get loose I mean didn't you say ..."

Before Kalaya could finish her sentence I took Stephan's hand and walked to the dance floor.

For the next couple of songs, we were looking into each other's eyes especially when the slow Music came on.

"Stacy I what you too I have been watching since you and your friends made your entrance. I said it before and I'd say it again you look very Sexy."

After he looked me in the eye and told me that a smile came across my face.

I felt my heart warming up and if he was capable of making this happen this was on Brother I'd have to get to know.

Rose had a name for all Men. We soon spotted a man in the corner we all could tell he was a Mama's boy no older than 25.

Now Mama Boys are what's up because those are the Men who'll treat you right. They know how to make a Woman happy. The only thing was we couldn't tell if he was mature enough to be a man or if was he still a boy. I quickly turned my head when he saw me looking at him and took another sip of my drink.

"Stacy look out! Because that last guy you were eyeing is headed our way." Kalaya said.

Within seconds he was in my face. "I noticed you were staring at me and I want to tell you straight up you look Sexy."

I quickly crossed my legs as if I didn't want to be bothered.

"Would you like to dance? And by the way, my name is Stephan what's yours?"

I had to admit he even looked better up close, but a sister has to play hard to get.

"You must think you're Mister Valentine, don't you? I'm tired of you men thinking the earth revolves around you."

Clam down Sister all I'm asking is for a dance. Look why don't I buy you and you're girls a drink? I mean I know you had you're drinks already but this one's on me.

Also, I'd like to see you smile. I mean there playing LL Cool J's new song from his 10th Album 'Luv You Better.'

"He's right Girl you need to get loose I mean didn't you say ..."

Before Kalaya could finish her sentence I took Stephan's hand and walked to the dance floor.

For the next couple of songs, we were looking into each other's eyes especially when the slow Music came on.

"Stacy I what you too know I've been watching you since you and your friends made your entrance. I said it before and I'd say it again you look very Sexy."

After he looked me in the eye and told me that a smile came across my face.

I felt my heart warming up and if he was capable of making this happen this was on Brother I'd have to get to know.

Rose had a name for all Men. We soon spotted a man in the corner we all could tell he was a Mama's boy no older than 25.

Now Mama Boys are what's up because those are the Men who'll treat you right. They know how to make a Woman happy. The only thing was we couldn't tell if he was mature enough to be a man or if was he still a boy. I quickly turned my head when he saw me looking at him and took another sip of my drink.

"Stacy look out! Because that last guy you were eyeing is headed our way." Kalaya said.

Within seconds he was in my face. "I noticed you were staring at me and I want to tell you straight up you look Sexy."

I quickly crossed my legs as if I didn't want to be bothered.

"Would you like to dance? And by the way, my name is Stephan what's yours?"

I had to admit he even looked better up close, but a sister has to play hard to get.

"You must think you're Mister Valentine, don't you? I'm tired of you men thinking the earth revolves around you."

"Clam down Sister all I'm asking is for a dance. Look why don't I buy you and you're girls a drink? I mean I know you had your drinks already but this one's on me. Also, I'd like to see you smile. I mean there playing LL Cool J's new song from his 10ᵗʰ Album 'Luv You Better.'"

"He's right Girl you need to get loose I mean didn't you say ..."

Before Kalaya could finish her sentence I took Stephan's hand and walked to the dance floor.

For the next couple of songs, we were looking into each other's eyes especially when the slow Music came on.

walked to the dance floor.

"Stacy I what you too I have been watching since you and your friends made your entrance. I said it before and I'd say it again you look very Sexy."

After he looked me in the eye and told me that a smile came across my face.

I felt my heart warming up and if he was capable of making this happen this was on Brother I'd have to get to know.

3

Kalaya

It was a little after 2:00 a.m. Rose and I was still at the bar while Katrina and Rose were still enjoying themselves with those Brothers.

"I had to admit that dared Katrina was dancing with wasn't bad looking at all.' Rose and I quickly continued our conversation. "Rose, what you said earlier you weren't serious were you?"

She gave me a serious look saying… "Kalaya you damn right I was serious about what I said and you of all people should know I was serious."

I continued to listen to what she was saying.

"You've got use these Nigger's for what they got or take what you can get, and you know I don't need no Nigger's money I mean I have a great job at the Post Office I pay my rent and Bills. I mean half of these Nigger's anit even got jobs out here but that's ok because I understand Society's been messed up since 9/11 and the other half just refuse to work.

"Rose the Lord might have blessed us with great jobs and Careers and that's good and all but he hasn't blessed us with a Man. I mean I'm tired of being the other woman I…I just want a man for myself."

Rose immediately shook her head saying… " Kalaya that' you're problem now. You're too caught up in this love shit. I mean you're right about one thing God did bless us with great jobs and all but this isn't the 60's or 70's where you had hard-working men coming home to support their families.

That's why I don't depend on a Nigger for shit.

As I watched Rose take another sip of her drink she continued by saying...

"Kalaya you know me better than anybody you know what my Stepfather Michael did to me. I mean don't you remember me crying because my Mother punched me in the face accusing me of fucking her Man while she was at work. And I looked up to Michael like a father."

Before Rose could even finish I cut her off because it had come back to me.

I could still picture her face the tears coming down her eyes.

We were in our senior year of Junior High School back then.

'Give a detail'

"Hey look girl Katrina's headed our way. I said

As I watched Katrina come to the bar she told us the Brother who she was dancing with name was Hasson and that they exchanged numbers.

"Ok, girl give us some details." Kalaya said.

Katrina just smiled at us. "There aren't any details to give, but while we were dancing he did tell me how much he appreciated a woman who didn't feel she needed to show off her body or advertise her looks all the time to get attention. Now if you two will excuse me I'm going to the Lady's room."

I could tell Katrina was holding back but it was all good as long as she was enjoying herself.

Moments later Stacy came through the crowd holding this Brother's hand.

"Ladies I'd like to introduce you to Stephan. Stephan this is Kalaya, Katrina, and Rose."

Stephan quickly shook our hands I had to admit this Brother wasn't bad-looking at all.

"So the way was it Stacy you approached earlier and not one of these Hoochies in here. I mean this is the Club where you men like to get you're one-night stands on right?"

"Rose!" Stacy shouted out.

We all looked at Rose. We had no clue as to why attacked Stephan like that, but it didn't bother him at all he just smiled at us. Well, Ladies as I told Stacy when I approached her she looks beautiful, and know offense to the other sisters in here but most of them have issues up in here. But you're girl Stacy is so attractive I just had to introduce myself." Stephan said as he kissed Stacy on the cheek.

After Stacy and Stephan exchanged numbers we were all ready to leave.

It was already 3:30 a.m. and usually, we'd be out of the club by 1:00 or 2:00 a.m.

As we exited the Club it was obvious Stacy was pretty upset. "Damn Rose you didn't have to attack him like that. I mean was that necessary?" Stacy asked.

"Look I'm sorry I was just testing him. Look I didn't want to see any of you get hurt because you'll know most Women give their bodies away thinking a man is going to commit to them. Also, I don't want to see any of you dating these Bulldogs out here."

After listening to Rose say that she quickly explained to us that a Bulldog was a man who hit on women or a man who must have his way all the time. She even explained to Stacy and Katrina the situation with her Mother and stepfather.

"And the Motherfucker started abusing my Mother and sleeping with other Women and my Mother was still in love with him. That's why I promised myself I'd never be that weak."

As I kept listening to what Rose was saying both Stacy and Kalaya had shocking looks on their faces.

Rose, we're sorry to hear that, but we're grown women now and you need to stop thinking every relationship is going to lead to Infidelity. As for your Mother that was years ago and if you want it you can get help for that but only if you want it. I mean didn't we just go to a play and Clubbing come on girl remember what we said it's to find our Mister Right." Stacy said.

"Yeah, whatever! I should have known you wouldn't understand because you haven't been through what I've been through. But thanks for the ride home Stacy I'll talk to you later and Katrina it was good seeing you again."

With those words said we all watched Rose enter her building and I had to say to myself Heaven help her.

4

Rose

By the time I unlocked my door, I quickly settled down ready to jump in the shower.

I always loved smelling fresh no matter what time I'd come home.

I always made sure my body and hair were clean. 30 Minutes later I had set my alarm clock to 10:00 am although I was very tired I couldn't wait until it was time for Church in the AM and praise God.

It was Sunday morning and I was in St. Anthony's Church listening to the Choir sing 'What A mighty God we serve.' I immediately open my and look up in the sky with a big smile on my face.

I had just started going back to Church after Michael and I had broken up 4months ago in January.

Michael and I dated each other for 3 years, but it came to an end when I found out he was a Drug dealer at night and day.

I remembered it all too well. The things he was saying and what he did to me when I wanted him to confess to me. "So Michael when were you going to tell me about these Drugs you've been selling."

"What are you talking about? Who the fuck told you about that? How did you find out?"

You mean you don't remember selling in front of Kalaya's building. Michael, you sold Drugs to one of her ex-men and Kalaya came and told me because she was right there in the Nigger's car. She even told me how she saw you kissing another woman. What's up with that Michael?"

"Look, babe, I'm sorry but you no times have been rough for me since 9/11.

"You know I should've been working for the MTA but after 9/11 they just went on a freeze and despite that, I had to drop out of school because of the money I owed them. Babe, please understand I've been selling these Drugs and saving up

money so I can finish up my last semester for my BA degree, and I'm still looking for work but everything is just fucked up right now."

For a moment I just looked at this Nigger like he was crazy. Because either he was looking to get himself killed or locked up.

"Michael there are other ways to handle that you've got to keep looking dam it Michael there are jobs out here. You should've come to me in the first place. I mean common sense should've told you ..."

Before I could say another word Michael punched me in my face giving me a black eye and started choking me. That was one Christmas I didn't want to enjoy with my friends or family. However, I did have Michael arrested for assault because it reminded me of when James would beat my Mother and I just couldn't deal with that. I always promised myself I'd never be that weak and think that if a man put his hands on you it was love. But that was four months ago now I was in the house of God serving him.

One hour later I was getting ready for Travis to stop by and cook for me. Travis was a cool brother he'd always stop by at least two Sundays a month just to see how I was doing. Travis was 5-10 with a nice and smooth caramel complexion.   He had black eyes and always kept himself in shape. The one reason why we never dated was because he was a No-Cash Brother. He'd have a job here and there and something bad would always happen.

Moments later Travis was at my house giving me one of his lectures. "Rose being home on a Sunday isn't always cool. Don't you ever bored?"

I just giggled at Travis saying... "Sometimes I get bored but I'm cool with my life. I have a great career and my own, place and I have my own money. But there's one thing missing." I couldn't believe what I just said."

Travis already knew what I was missing in my life. I could tell he was always waiting for me to say it to him.

"Rose you don't have to be ashamed to say it."

"Say what Travis?"

"You know what I'm talking about. I mean ever since you broke up with Michael it's like you isolated yourself from others. I mean sure you have a good life and a great job but that's nothing if you don't have someone to share it with."

"Travis, what are you trying to say?"

I mean this No-Cash Brother was on the money. I did have everything a woman can ask for except that one thing and that was a man and I mean a man to laugh with and enjoy life with. For the past few months, I'd been caught up in seeking revenge on Men I never thought about what Travis was trying to say.

"Travis you think you know me. Do you know how I feel right now?"

"No Rose, I don't, but I do feel like you deserve the love of a good Black Man like myself. I'm talking about a man that cares about you, a man that can always talk the talk and walk the walk. Most of all Rose you need a man that's going to give you his all."

"Shut up!" I squealed as I stepped away from him. "Just shut up already." Travis did exactly what I said and started tonguing me down.

For the next 10 minutes, we were exploring each other with kisses. Travis quickly unbuttoned my bra and started sucking my nipples. Within seconds I had provided Travis

With access to enter my walls and as he gazed into my eyes saying…
"I'm going to make your body feel so good and…"

"Travis enough."   I was quickly turned off. I was one of those Sisters who loved a man when he took his time and got to know my body.

"Travis maybe this wasn't. ohhh."

Before I could finish my sentence Travis had entered my walls and I had to admit it felt good.

Later that evening, Travis was on the phone asking the same question he asked earlier.

"Travis I'm sorry but we can't see each other regularly.

I mean you're a Brother who loves coming home to that special woman and

I'm just not that woman."

There was silence over the phone. I was hoping I didn't hurt his feelings but

He had to know the truth. "Look Travis I'm just being honest with you."

"Rose it's all right I understand we are from two different worlds. Look, Rose, I'm going to get ready for my test with Con Edison tomorrow, but promise me something promise me you're going to get some tips on counseling. I mean the way you play with men's hearts isn't right at all."

"Excuse me?"

"Look all I'm saying is when real love comes you're the way you're not going to do with that person because you say pushing good men out of your life. Take care of yourself, Rose."

As I hung up the phone I started thinking about what Travis said. I had no idea Travis was interested in Con Edison. I was happy for him because it showed me that Travis was a quitter but I just hope he understood that it would never happen between me and him.

I called Kalaya to talk about the last statement Travis made but she didn't pick up the phone so I just left a message.

When I looked at the time it was 11:50 and I knew it was time to get ready for my shower because I had to be at work at 6:00 am. I went in the shower still thinking about what Travis said to me earlier. I knew I wouldn't open up to just anyone. The person would have to be someone I'm really into and feel.

Hood Lover

5
Rose

I was just about ready to take my lunch break. I had two more people online ready to do priority mail.

This was my second year working as a Mail Clerk. I was ready to take the supervisor's test and move up with my career at the Post Office.

"Hello Excuse me! I'd like to Mail this Priority please."

Wow! This brother was fine I noticed most Women in the lobby were staring at this man including the one behind him.

He stood about six feet even. He had a brown-skinned complexion with black eyes and the suit he was wearing was the boom.

"Hello, beautiful my name is Charles Powell. Are you sure you should be working in the Post Office or out somewhere Modeling?"

"Excuse me! Look I take Pride in what I do and...."

"Relax! Clam down all I'm saying is you look real good."

I started smiling but not because of his compliment. I quickly reminded him he had to have an address of where the mail was going. Another slow-ass nigga I thought he might be one of those Brothers who lacks common sense, but that wasn't stopping me from looking him up and down.

After I helped the Lady behind him I was ready for Lunch, but Charles came back to my window asking me to mail his letter priority.

"You never did tell me you're name."

"Was I supposed to?"

You don't have to if you don't want to. I understand you're at work and you're keeping it at a professional level. So just maybe you'd tell me you're name if I came to see you Model and I'll say it to you again you look good."

I couldn't help but blush this time. My name's Rose and I'm getting ready to go to Lunch thank you." I said as I walked away from my counter.

Moments later as I walked out of the Post Office ready to get something to eat Charles was walking right beside me still trying to throw his lines at me he told me he was a Correction Officer and that he had never seen a beautiful Post Office Clerk.

If he thought these lines were going to win me over he was right.

Before I watched him get into his Lexus Rx 300 he had given me his number and address asking me to house for dinner on Thursday on his off day.

Three days later I was in my bedroom fixing my hair and nails getting ready for my dinner date with Charles. I didn't tell any of the girls about him because I wanted to find out what Charles had to offer. I gave Charles my address on Wednesday night and as I was doing my nails the doorbell rang.

For once I meant a man that can come on time. "Just a minute!" I yelled out as I was putting my nail polish away.

As I opened the door I quickly stared at Charles up and down getting a good look at him. He had on

"Here these are for you. Damn girl, I didn't expect you to look this damn good you got it going on."

"And don't you forget it." I said as I accepted the roses he gave me.

We quickly started exploring each other with kisses. Which led to him kissing my neck but I quickly put on the brakes. You see people my neck was one of my weak spots because it always made me ready to get my shit off.

I was so surprised at how much of a gentleman Charles was it turned things around I wasn't even thinking about using him or seeing what I could get out of him. Instead, I wanted to everything about him.

One hour later both Charles and I were feeding each other Black Cherry Ice Cream, and every time I fed him he would reward me with a long kiss.

It was as if Charles was trying to make me the best date of his adult life.

"Come here babe let me feed you with these two Cherry and we can put the Strawberry elsewhere later."

"Relax yourself, man! I   mean is that all you men think of is getting in a woman's jeans?"

"Ha...Ha....Ha... Sorry Rose but you look good girl even when you get angry."

"I'm not angry. I'm just not one of those Sisters who you're going to use as a Stastic."

"Look I can't speak for those other men out there and I can't change my past but

I can tell you I'm a man who respects you. I mean I respect everything about you already you're mind body and soul everything. Even when I'm not around you I'll be with you in Spirit everywhere."

With that being said I let myself fall into his arms as he carried me into his bedroom.

It was Friday night and I was waiting for Charles's arrival. I was thinking about tonight all day at work. Because of the way he worked my body at his apartment that was something I will never forget. I started imagining what it would feel like to be in a real relationship with Charles. Could I trust him? Should I use him? Should I just make him a fuck buddy? Lord help me I said to myself.

When Charles entered my apartment I was amassed at how fine he was looking.

He took the dress to impress to another level. I quickly put on some music as I gave him a tour of my apartment. "Nice pictures."

As we walked back into the living room Charles was telling me how much he loved African Art.

Within seconds we were both lying on my couch as his fingers were stroking through my hair Charles quickly started telling me his life story and why he became a Correction Officer.

As I kept listening to Charles's story tears started coming down my eyes. "No more please Charles I don't want to hear anymore."

"What's wrong babe?"

"It must have been really hard growing up without your mother."

Yeah! It was hard but I looked at it as a positive instead of a negative. Rose, I've known my Mother for 7 years and my Father raised me the best way he could and I still thank God for that every day."

As I was headed to the kitchen ready to start dinner Charles came in telling me he wanted a woman that is going to be his best friend and his future Soul mate. I was totally surprised and caught off guard but I quickly put my lips to his as he started to carry me to my bedroom.

"Wait, babe, what about dinner?"

"I didn't forget because you're about to feed me now!"

Within seconds Charles started to gently rub my thighs and as his fingers were

rubbing my breast. It had been a very long time since someone touched my body the way Charles did. I was very surprised at the way he was taking his time with my body. Charles started kissing my thighs and before I could let out a moan his tongue had already entered me.

Moments later. "I'm about to come ohh…ohh."

I didn't want Charles to stop I kept my hands on his head as I kept moaning.

"No don't stop babe!"

Relax babe I'm just going to get my rubbers."

Wow! For a minute there I thought Charles wanted me to return the favor not that I wouldn't but the way his tongue felt was damn good.

Knock!!

As Charles came back in my room he told me someone was at my door and that I should answer it. I wondered who the hell could be at my door this late. It was 12:30 am my girlfriends knew I had to work in the mourning. As I looked through the peephole my mood quickly changed. 'Shit! What the hell is he doing here?'

A smile came on his face once I opened the door.

"Babe girl what's been going on?"

"Michael, what the hell are you doing here?"

'Don't you people hate it when an ex comes by unannounced especially when you've got company and the night is going so well?'

I was going to call but decided to come here and talk with you in person.

Michael whispered in my ear. "I want to make your body real hot so take your nightgown off. Because I never felt the way I do about making love to you tonight."

"Michael I told you we're through, now I think it's best that you leave before I call the cops."

His facial expression quickly changed. "Look, Rose, you know I love you and I'm letting you know I'm not leaving here until we talk things over. Babe put your trust in me There's no other place I'd rather be than be here with you. "Now are you going to let me in or what?"

'Who the Hell did he think he was talking to?' "Is there a problem here babe?" Charles said as he came to the door in his boxes.

"And who the hell are you one of her Boy Scouts?"

Charles was about to take a swing on Michael but I managed to jump in front of him I quickly told Michael I'd call 911 if he didn't leave. I wanted to press charges on him just for eyeing me down head to toe.

"Look, Rose, it's been a long time and I feel like we should try our love again.

I mean I miss that smile of yours and most of all I miss the way you make me feel."

"What?"

'The nerve of this man did he actually think I would forget about what he did to me I may forgive but I most certainly don't forget.'

Michael, it's time for you to leave. I said as I grabbed Charles's arm just to let him know who was getting this pussy tonight.

"I'm not leaving here until we talk about us," Michael said smiling at me.

Hood Lover

"Look I've had enough the lady asked you nicely to leave now I suggest you do that before I put my foot down your throat."

"Those some mighty big words you saying, bro. I hope you can back them up."

"Look Nigga I deal with punk mother fuckers like you every day."

"Look there will be no fighting here not at my door. I'm not trying to get kicked out of my apartment now Michael just leave. Charles let's go in the bedroom because I'm ready for some…"

I'm right behind you babe because that's my pussy." Charles said as he slammed the door shut in Michael's face.

As Charles closed the door I could hear Michael saying. 'This isn't over.'

6

Hassan

Sept 2006

I was in my office awaiting Katrina's call so we could go on our lunch date. Since meeting Katrina back in April I've had a bunch of smiles on my face no matter if a situation was good or bad. I worked at the Door there we help a lot of kids and young adults have a positive attitude toward life.

Katrina told me all about her problems with her ex-finance and the things he put her through. One of them was her inability to trust, love, and care for another man.

I could never forget the night we met each other. Before we exchanged numbers I told her I had just gotten back the courage to love again. Therefore she shouldn't be afraid to love again. I could never forget the way her eyes lit up when I said that statement.

I explained to her there are several reasons why men cheat. "Some men have She quickly turned the subject around asking... "So why do men cheat?"

Some men have issues just like women. Some do just for the fun of it and for the women who deal with men who cheat some may feel like they can't get another man."

I remembered it well people because the way Katrina folded her arms when I said that statement made it seem as if I was hosting a TV show. I quickly told her that some women may stay with the cheating man because they have nowhere else to live or they may want to keep their family together.

"Another reason why some men cheat is because of their pride. They may feel like they can't handle commitment and then some may feel like they must have more than one woman."

"Oh really!"

"Clam down Katrina and just listen because you do have some real Brothers out here such as myself. Some men may be faithful as hell only to find out the woman whom they've been faithful to was cheating on them. And for that reason, the faithful man becomes a Player all because he's afraid of getting hurt again."

After I said that statement I pulled out my new Cell phone giving her the number and the number to my house. I let her know she can call me anytime and any day. She quickly gave me her number and said the same thing.

As I continued to think about the time Katrina and I met at the club. I quickly cracked a smile because of the smile I put on her face that night.

Knock! "Come in."

"Hasson you have a call on line 2." Kim said.

Kim was a nice brown-skinned woman with a slim body. Kim was an administrative assistant at the Door she weighed about 120 and stood about 5,7 and although Kim was fine as hell I did not mix business with pleasure.

"Hasson speaking who's this?"

"Hi, babe what's up?"

"Shantel, what do you want out of my life?"

"Nothing except you haven't been calling me these last few weeks. I thought we had something going, babe."

"Shantel we've been through this already I was loyal, and caring and my heart was sensitive, but you chose to be with another man because he has a car."

"Wait! Wait! Babe that was a mistake."

I laughed after she said that. "Look Shantel another reason I've put you out of my life is because I was tired of you provoking me. I was tired of you on the phone and telling your friends I'm a nobody and I was tired of going to your house and coming home feeling like I was ready to kill people.

"So what happened the last time between us meant nothing?"

No, Shantel, it meant nothing at all. Now if you'll excuse me I'm expecting a call from Katrina, my new woman. And Shantel she respects what I do for a living. Remember a good woman stands by her man when he treats her right. I said as I hung up the phone. It didn't matter to me if I hurt Shantel's feelings or not because I was looking forward to being with the new woman in my life.

My cell had gone off the moment I hung up the phone

"Finally." I said to myself because I didn't need any more drama in my life.

Since Katrina, and I started seeing each other every co-worker or close friend of mine has noticed the smiles I've had on my face just about every day. Katrina and I had met each other for lunch a few times as we continued getting to know each other. As I walked out the door and saw Katrina our lips quickly connected.

"Hi, babe. Where do you want to eat today?" Katrina asked.

"Well, babe I've got a lot of work to do so well just go to dinner Amell across the street," I said as I took her by the hand leading her toward the restaurant.

Moments later as we were at the table having lunch. "Hasson I want you to help plan my parent's 25th anniversary in September because this year is going to be one to remember." Katrina said as she stuffed her face with macaroni.

Babe it'll be my pleasure helping you plan their wedding anniversary, I must thank them for creating such a beautiful woman." I said as I continued to look her in the eye.

30 minutes later as we were walking out of the restaurant I noticed 3 teenage guys in front of the door. One had a box cutter to Kevin's throat screaming… "I want my money! Mother fucker don't even think you're getting off that easy"

I quickly kissed Katrina and told her I'd call her later. As I was waiting for the light to change I saw the other guy with braids in his hair punch Kevin in the face and knock him to the ground. He quickly pulled out a blade looking down at Kevin screaming where's the funds Nigger.

As the light turned green I immediately ran across the street asking is there was a problem. The guy with braids quickly looked at me saying… "Be easy dread this doesn't concern you. This is strictly business your boy here owes my boy here some funds now where is it, Kevin?"

I quickly told all three of them that whatever Kevin owes any one of you it's not worth killing him, and it's not worth going to jail for. "That's what's wrong with us now we're too busy killing each other. And getting locked up, that's why you have more and more black females in College and least black males."

"And who are you our father? Yo dread I told you go ahead with that bullshit bro this doesn't concern you."

"It does concern me when I see one of our members here rooming the streets. And I'm letting all three of you know I can help all three of you even though you aren't members I can still help you, but you will have to trust me."

"I didn't seem to get through to them because the one with the blade kept pointing it at Kevin saying "Remember what I said you'd better have my money. And you still owe me 2 ounces Nigger."

After I heard that I knew what was going on and I told Kevin and a bunch of other young adults at my job about getting involved with those types of people, That was the reason I brought him here in the first place.

I never forgot about how it finally caught up with my brother.

It was 12 years ago when me and my mother came home from my basketball game in high school.

My Mother broke down crying when she saw her oldest son lying dead in front of her door.

I still remember what the copy of the letter said.

'Richie you're lying you lying dead on the ground for not giving me my pound. You thought I would let you take my money and let you take my money and not give me my pound. But I still love you I just wanted you to feel the pain I felt when I lost our baby due to that miscarriage. I also wanted you to feel the pain I felt after you dumped me but Richie it's a good thing you died in the Hood because you'll always be my Hood Lover. Goodbye, Richie, and remember all Dogs go to Heaven rest in peace.

At the time I was glad when the cops caught that crazy bitch Sabrina, but that motivated me into helping other young males and females stay positive towards life and not get caught up in the Drug game. Because so many of our young Brothers and Sisters are letting the streets get the best of them these days.

Since graduating from York College I've devoted myself to helping Children and Young Adults. I pray that one day I'll be able to start my own Nonprofit Organization that helps our children.

3 Weeks later I was in Manhattan Mall with Katrina picking out a gift for her parent's Wedding Anniversary.

She was so excited to be planning their Anniversary. Katrina explained to me how she and her parents became close again.

"Oh, babe look at that it's so beautiful." Katrina said pulling me towards her.

It was an African art drawing with a man holding the earth and a picture with a man purposing to a woman "Babe we should also get your Mom and Dad Wedding Anniversary card."

"Hasson you pick it out while I go to Victoria's Secret and pick something out."

I was curious about what she was going in there to buy, but I quickly spotted the perfect anniversary card it said 'Still in love with you.'

Moments later after I paid for the card Katrina suggested that we both take a picture together. Now usually I'd tell a woman no but Katrina had become that special woman in my life in just a short period. Katrina had beauty, she was smart, loyal, and caring, and she loved helping people, especially kids. A smile quickly came on my face it was as if God was letting me know she was my other half but only time would tell.

After we were done in the mall I was at my place cooking dinner for my lady out in Queens Bridge Projects I was making Fried Chicken with white rice and green beans.

As we sat at the table eating she stood up asking me to give my own opinion of the most important thing in a relationship.

"What do you mean babe?" 'Because when women ask a question like this it means they're trying to figure the two of you stand in the relationship you're in.'

"What do I mean? I mean how do you think my parents and other couples stay married or be together for so long?"

I knew where this was going because even though I had gained Katrina's trust in just a short period she still had insecurities in her all because of her past.

The first time she told me everything was going to be alright with us for now because the relationship was fresh. She also asked how I'd feel about her 3 years from now.

I told her that 3 years from now I'm going to love her more and more and as the years go on my love for her will be stronger and stronger no matter how many arguments or problems we face. I also said to her to take life day by day so I was prepared for this conversation. Because the time I was single I gave myself time to heal and get my life together and it made me a better man.

"Hasson, are you really in love with me? Because I have to know if you're ready for this kind of commitment."

Babe with all due respect to you I'm starting to think you're a little too dense because you keep asking the same thing."

I quickly grabbed her by the waist saying… "Katrina babe I'm in love with you and I want you to know I'm not going anywhere. I mean…"

I paused for a second or two then said… "Katrina I want you to realize I'm going to want to marry you someday."

" What?"

I quickly put both our plates in the sink as I started to wash the dishes, and I looked at her telling her how I wanted us to start a family someday.

The look I got from her wasn't a bad one but I had to be sure where her head was so I used reverse psychology asking her doesn't she wanted to have children with me someday so we could grow old together.

Katrina quickly hugged me and we both started exploring each other with kisses.

"Relax Hasson I'm going to take a shower now. But babe be ready for the best sex of your life. As Katrina jumped in the shower I heard the phone ringing and went to answer it. "Hello!"

"Hey, Hasson it's me, Chris. I'm tired of going through the bullshit with these women out here especially mine. I mean I'm tired of her accusing me of cheating on her because all of this shit is making me unhappy. Hasson you know I stopped being that guy fucking 2 Or 3 women a day or every other day. Hasson do you know how many women I've turned down, I'm talking about real women with great jobs who have their place and want more out of life. Not to mention every last one of them asked me to move in with them, and I've turned every one of them down."

"Ok! Chris ok! I hear you but I think you forgotten that you had sex with 2 of her best friends and that was only a month ago in August. And don't you remember her friend Jennifer came telling her how great the sex you two had was? Bro, you can't be upset with your lady because of her suspicions because when a woman's fed up with you can do 2 things. One you can leave or you can face her and just deal with insecurities."

"You telling me I should put up with her insecurities."

"Chris is honest with yourself and Thresh."

Before I could say another word Katrina came into the bedroom combing her hair and wearing purple thongs. "Chris I'll talk with you later bro but remember what I said tell her how feel. Just be honest with her I'll talk with you at work long enjoy your weekend."

I quickly started staring Katrina in her eyes telling her how sexy she was we both gazed into each other's eyes as our lips connected with each other's.

"Have patience Hasson and lay down, I'm in control this time."

As she unbuttoned her bra I quickly took one of her breasts into my hand pulling it up into my mouth.

And as Katrina pulled off her thongs she quickly let the head of my dick into her walls. She exhaled for one moment and then started riding. She started grabbing my chest as she kept going at a fast pace. As she continued to ride me I took hold of one of her hands and had my other palming her ass and as she kept riding me she gave me a sign telling me she was ready to cum. Even her moans were telling me she was ready to cum.

"Ohh! Hasson Ohhh!"

We quickly started kissing each other and this time our kisses were even more electrifying, but Katrina stood me up telling me she wanted it from the back.

Minutes later she went back to riding me and this time going faster than before we made love the rest of the night. Our moans were louder than before and we both came.

"Oh! I love you, Hasson."

"I love you too Katrina and don't you ever forget that."

With that being said she collapsed on my chest as we both fell asleep.

7

Katrina

The next morning Hassan and I were at it again. To the readers reading this you'll know how that mourning sex is right.

"Oh! Babe that feels so good." Hasson kept sucking my nipples and the more he sucked them the more I was ready to let out that big explosion. I loved the way Hasson always took his time with my body he worked his way down to my thighs and then started fingering and playing with my pussy.

"Unh-uh." My body began to tremble because the things Hasson was doing to my body had my mind going elsewhere.

"Relax babe I haven't done anything yet, but moaning like that you're bound to get this."

"Uhhh!" Hasson quickly had me open my legs and put his tongue to work.

10 Minutes later Katrina was holding Hasson's head because of the way his tongue was working her body was feeling good.

It was as if he was trying to spell his was doing its work. Making her body tremble. Hasson quickly looked me in the eye letting me know he wanted to make sure I get as much pleasure from this lovemaking as he was. His tongue went straight into my mouth and we were toasting and turning in my bed tonguing each other down.

"Hasson let me ride you."

"Of course, my queen whatever pleases you pleases me."

Man! In my whole adult life, I never heard a man say that. I gazed into his eyes and buried my tongue in his mouth and started riding him as I never did before because I wanted to prove to him that I had some good pussy to give him.

As I continued to ride Hasson this time going faster and faster he started to squeeze my breast and I quickly lowered them allowing him to suck on my nipples.

Minutes later we were doing it Doggy Style one of my favorite positions.

It wasn't just a Bump and grind I mean… 'Well, ladies you know how it is working your body and pulling your hair.'

Hasson's manhood was buried inside of me I can't remember the last time I been this wet.

As we continued doing it Doggy style I could feel the head of his manhood getting deeper and deeper as the two of us were enjoying the energetic sex that was in the room.

30 Minutes later the two of us collapsed on Hasson's bed giggling and smiling while holding each other. "Hasson I love you." I said. "I love you too my queen as he buried his tongue in my mouth."

Moments later as the two of us came out of the shower together we were discussing my parent's wedding anniversary because I wanted everything to go right for them.

"Now remember Hasson I'll be here at 7:00 pm because I want us to ride the train together on our way there."

"I thought when you ride me it is just me and you."

"Shut up you clown," I said as I kissed him goodbye letting him know to be ready when I got here.

Later that afternoon I was getting ready for the big night for my Parents.

"Come on Katrina you can do this," I said to myself as I was feeling my hair and dress.

I knew my aunt would be there with her husband Fred and her daughter Andrea who was like a sister to me. We hadn't seen each other in over 2 years and even though it was my parent's Wedding Anniversary I wanted to show all of them the new me. Only my parents saw me here and there but they never saw their daughter in the Black light-fuel dress I had on. No one has seen me in it since I brought it because I was saving it for something big like this.

This was a night I was looking forward to it was my parent's Wedding Anniversary and most of all it was the first time they'd be meeting Hasson.

"When I arrived at Hasson's house it was fifth teen minutes to six.

Hasson let's go you can put that Vanilla oil in you're in dreads when we get on the train."

"Relax babe I'm just putting my shoes on." Hasson said as his lips quickly connected with mine.

"I see you decided to go all out Hasson with that leisure suit maybe I should start calling you my Pimp instead of my man."

"Katrina you shouldn't even talk with that sexy black dress you have on. What are you trying to look sexy to remind me about the woman I have?"

"Ha! Ha! Very funny."

"There's nothing funny coming out of my mouth because you have my full attention. Babe, you have my full attention, and this is a Sean John Italian Suit I have on. And it's to remind you the kind of man you have and what he's all about."

Hasson said as I watched him start me up and down.

"Babe, you look delicious tonight, as a matter of fact, why don't you feed me right now."

"I mean you know what they say if the juice is sweet keep tasting it."

Hasson quickly started kissing my ear and neck and it was quickly taking me to another place."Oh no, you don't." I said as I stood up off the couch telling him it was time to go.

"Babe let's have a quickie before we leave."

And get my hair messed up Hasson it's already 5 minutes past six. Besides the last time, we called ourselves having a quickie we were in the bedroom for 2 hours and I was late for school and you were for work. Now for the last time let's go."

As Hasson and I entered the train station at Queens Bridge we ran into his friend Chris. Hasson showed me a picture of Chris at his apartment.

Chris quickly walked up to me saying… "Now you must be Katrina I've heard a lot about you. Allow me to introduce myself I'm Chris" Chris said as he kissed my hand.

"Chris, what are you doing here?"

"I'm sorry but I had to get out of the house I'm tired of these phone calls I've been getting, and these women saying I've misled them.

I mean Barbara just left my house talking about how I've misled her."

"Most likely you did."

"Whatever Nigger! She knows I'm still with Tresha and she and her just got into an argument because she called when Barbara was there and she heard us arguing. I mean Hasson I'm just tired of all this arguing. That's why I came out here just to get away from all the bullshit."

I watched Hasson shake his head saying... "First of all why did you even pick up the phone when Barbara was there? That was your first mistake."

"Excuse me, Hasson!" I said as I folded my arms waiting to hear what he had to say.

"Relax babe I'm just having a Man to Man talk with Chris. You know babe a Brother to Brother talk. Now Chris what the Hell is going on with you man I thought you stopped fucking around with these women's emotions I mean when are you going to realize you're not God's gift to women."

"I never said I was, But they surely make me feel that way. Look, Hasson, why don't I come with you two? By the way, where are you going is it a night for two."

"No Chris we are going to my Parent's Wedding anniversary party and sure you can come all my girlfriends will be there and my close relatives will be there. Besides you look like you could get away from the Hood for a while."

As we were riding the F train I was listening to what Chris had to say.

"I'm telling you guys I've just got this feeling like Trisha is seeing someone else."

"Chris you're being ridiculous and you know it. Trisha is in love with you and you know it."

"Come on Hasson you no 9 out of ten times the one who accuses their partner of cheating is normally the one who doing the cheating." Chris said.

Before any of us could say another word Hasson and I watched this tall black sister come up on Chris pointing her finger in his face saying... "First of all, it's because of you men that women cheat."

Chris quickly jumped up out of his seat saying… "First of all you shouldn't be in my business second I'm making up for what happened with me and my lady first started dating."

"Why now because she is ready to run off with the next man?" The woman said as she got off the train.

I watched Chris's face begin to boil but I was glad that he was not letting his anger get the best of him.

"Look I'm sorry if this offends you but if you want to know why you have women cheating these days. 1 Either they've been cheated on too many times and are just tired of the male bullshit. 2 there looking for their mister to do right so that's why you have women going from guy to guy to find out which one has and makes the most money, and most of the times that's the man they stay with. Usually, that's the man they stay with because that man can pay their bills and do whatever for them.

As I continued explaining to Chris and Hasson why you have women cheating on their men these days.

"Chris you've got to understand most women these days cheat because of the opportunity they have. A lot of them are not satisfied with the man they are with, and Chris you also have women being influenced by other women, and most of the time that woman doesn't have a man so she would want her girl to be miserable or lonely like she is. Another reason why she may influence her girlfriend to cheat is because she wants that man for herself."

"Oh really! Are you speaking from experience?"

I had to exhale after Chris asked me that question. "Yes Chris I'm talking from experience, but it's like Hover said on his song 'Anit no Nigger' Tell your friend to find a man of their own."

I quickly changed the subject by saying… "You know Chris what you need is a Vertical woman, and I have just the woman for you."

"Are you sure about this babe?" Hasson said.

"Oh shut up Hasson. Katrina who is you're friend you'd like to introduce me to."

"Yes, who is it babe I'm curious?"

I whispered in Hasson's ear who it was.

"Hey, no secrets just tell me who it is?"

"Have patience Bro." Hasson said.

30 Minutes later as we got off the 3 Train at Bergen Street and headed to my parent's house I saw my Aunt inside the house. "Oh God!" I said.

"What's wrong babe?"

I explained to Hasson that was my Aunt and her daughter in that Lincoln Navigator that just passed us. I told Hasson about the jealousy between me and my Cousin. And to all you readers it was more of her being jealous of me because I grew out of that a long time ago. We approached my Parent's doorstep and I quickly introduced Hasson and Chris to my girlfriends. "It appears we all got here at the same time ladies. It's good to see you all again I'm glad you all could make it. Hey, Stacy where's Stephan? Don't tell me you did scare that man away already girl."

"No Katrina Stephan in the Studio tonight, but he told me to wish your parents a happy anniversary."

"Yeah my man Kenny had to work but he told me to tell your parents they are truly blessed."

"What!!" Stacy shouted out.

We all looked shocked to hear what Rose had just said to us about the new man in her life. Even I had thought she had given up on love.

Rose just smiled at us. "Yes ladies it's true I'm back in love again, but my guard is always up. Now forget about me this is about Katrina's parents' Wedding Anniversary so let's go inside now, please.

"Ummm, ummm." Chris came over and introduced himself kissing each one of my girlfriend's hand.

Kalaya's, hand was the last and I saw the way she looked at him from head to toe.

It looked like her tongue was ready to fall out of her mouth but that was just my opinion. Now that was a good thing because, at the end of the night, it wouldn't be a problem hooking the two of them up.

When we entered my parent's house I quickly went to give my Mother and Father a hug and kiss as well as my Aunt. I gave my Cousin, a look, but it was nothing like the look my Mother gave Stacy.

I knew what that look my Mother gave Stacy meant and that would turn things around. People you've got to understand I'm one of those people that believes black people can get together and have a good time. So the last thing I wanted to see was my Mother go off in here. I smiled at my Mother reminding her how much I love Mom let me introduce you to my man, my other half, my Soul Mate Hasson.

Hasson quickly extended his hand. "It's a pleasure to finally meet you, Mrs. Jefferson. Here this is for you and your Husband Happy Anniversary."

"Thank you, Hasson it's a pleasure to meet you too. My husband is upstairs putting away the gifts my sister brought us he'll be downstairs soon."

Chris walked up to my Mother kissing her and my Aunt and Cousin on their hand as he introduced himself I saw my cousin looking at Chris like she wanted to give him some. Soon everyone came over wishing my Mother and Father a happy anniversary.

As everyone got comfortable my Mother and Father already knew my girlfriends so seeing them was nothing new.

As we all watched my Mother and Father open their presents Hasson came over and gave them an anniversary card. Hasson and my Father quickly shook hands. "I never expected my daughter to be dating a guy with dreads. What you're religion Hasson?"

"Excuse me, sir."

Everyone started paying attention to what my father said a moment ago.

"Look, Mr. Hasson, I've been looking forward to meeting you so I can tell you to your face. I'm very protective of my daughter, especially after what happened with her last relationship."

"Daddy!!" I shouted out as I looked over at Stacy.

"I'm sorry princess but I'm concerned about the choices you make both professional and personal."

Hasson just stood there listening to my Father while everyone else was in shock to hear my Father talk like this.

"Excuse me! With all due respect to you Mr. Hill you're out of line." Chris said.

My Father got up out of his chair looking at everyone and right back at Hasson saying… "I'm sorry Hasson but what I'm trying to say is my daughter has a chance to go get her Business Law Degree again and get far in life and I don't want some punk to ruin my daughter's chances of life."

Hasson quickly got up out of his seat looking at my Father. "Alright, Mr. Hill you've made your point now it's my turn. Katrina knows me very well I already have my BA Degree in Business and I'm not some little street punk I work in …"

Enough! Enough! Hasson calm down babe Daddy we're all here to celebrate you and Mommy's Anniversary now can you please stop? I said as I went to hug Hasson to let my Parents know this was the man I'd hope to grow old with.

One hour later while we were all at the table having dinner. It had seemed like everyone clam down that was until my Cousin opened her mouth. Damn, what a bitch people.

"So Hasson where was it you said you worked at?"

'What! The nerve of this Lincoln Terrace park hoochie.'

Valerie was my first cousin we were about the same height except she was a little thinner than me. The Bitch had no reason to ask my man that kind of question.

"Yes! Hasson if you don't mind me asking what is it you do for a living and what are your plans for the future."

'What was this attack my man day.'

Everyone was waiting to hear what Hasson had to say. It was becoming frustrating for me but Hasson didn't even get upset instead he whipped his mouth off and said… "Mr. Hill with all due respect I don't see what this has to do with your because I don't have a problem sharing it with you.

I work at the Door both me and Chris D. There we help Teenagers and young adults with their school work. It's a program that helps kids from off the street, especially teenagers because you have so many of them joining these gangs out here and a lot of them are becoming parents out here at an early age."

"Yes but…"

Hasson quickly put his hand across the table saying… "Please if you don't mind Ms. Hill because I'm not finished," Hasson said to my Cousin.

"As I was saying I work as a Counselor and I'm a Mentor to the majority of the Kids and Teenagers that come there. Now I'll be glad to tell you my plans for the future because in 2007 I plan on opening my nonprofit Recreation because I take pride in helping others."

I almost started to laugh when I saw the look on everyone's face. I'm sure you readers thought that shut my Father u, but you are wrong.

He looked Hasson in his face saying… "Mr. Hasson how do you plan on raising and supporting a family."

"Look Mr. Hill I came here to meet you and you're a wife and celebrate your anniversary not to be interviewed for a job."

"People! People! Can't we all get along I swear most Black people can't go anywhere and have a good time."

My Aunt said as she put on Tony Tony's CD and played the song Anniversary perfect timing Auntie I said to myself.

That was a little too personal and I know my Cousin was enjoying this but it was time to put an end to this nonsense. My Parents are overprotective at times, especially Dad.

"Look Dad Hasson and I aren't thinking about having kids any time soon, in fact, Hasson always encourages me to finish school so I can practice Law. Can't you two see I'm happy?"

"You said that about the last guy you introduced us to." My Mom said.

"Yeah, you did what was his name again? Oh yeah, Darrin, that's it, Darrin." Dad said.

"Oh, Yeah Uncle that was his name." My cousin said.

After hearing that I got up from the table looking directly at my Cousin telling the bitch to mind her damn business.

Stacy, Kalaya, and Rose came up to me telling me they were leaving including Chris they all said their goodbye man this was not how I pictured celebrating my parent's anniversary.

At that moment I told Hasson it was time for us to leave. "I hope you are happy Mom and you too Dad not only did you embarrass me but you ruined your Wedding Anniversary we were all here to celebrate with you and Mom."

Instead of just going out the door Hasson walked up to my Mom, Aunt, and Cousin telling them it was nice meeting them and that's what I loved about him he was a true gentleman.

"Valerie if you ever bring up my past, and my business I will kick your black ass out.

Let's go, Hasson, I'll stay in Queens Bridge with you tonight and yes Dad it's Queens Bridge Projects."

We took a cab to Hasson's place and we were both quiet. Until Hasson told how sorry he was for what happened tonight.

I told him it was alright. Although it was my Parent's Anniversary this was one relationship they would have to accept.

8

Stephan

Being in the Studio is what I love, but sometimes it can be tiring. I have been working on tracks in the studio since 9:00 am and as I looked at my watch it was now 10:00 pm that's over 10 hours of hard work. Even though I was determined to finish these last two song's I needed a break. "Let's take five," I said to the A&R the Producer and the man doing the Label came telling me not to leave because we were almost finished.

I quickly straighten his ass out reminding him I was the one doing the work and putting out this Music and as I sat down I started thinking about Stacy. Stacy was the new woman in my life she was different not because of her race but because of her attitude toward life itself. I could tell she had a high IQ and was the tip not to take shit from a Nigga. Talking with Stacy always cleared my head of things that were going on in my life.

I picked up my Cell phone dialing Stacy's number.

"Hello!"

"Hello, Stacy what's going on with you? And why does it sound like you're crying?"

"Stephan, where are you? I need to see you because it was awful."

"I'm still at the Studio, but why are you crying? And what was awful?"

I listened to Stacy explain to me what happened at her girlfriend's Parent's house I started feeling bad for her. "I should've been there for you babe I'm sorry you had to go through that type of disrespect." I said.

I should've never talked her into going there alone without me being there to support her. As I was headed back to the Studio I told the Producer the beats and the A&R we'd have to finish these last Tracks tomorrow and what shacked was that they agreed with me. I could tell in their faces they were just as tired as I was one of the guys said he had a family to go home to and as for me, I had a woman that needed my comfort. As I was driving towards Stacy house I quickly turned to get in the left lane.

"Damn drive Mother Fucker."

Damn, don't these people no when you're in the left lane you're supposed to drive. I was really worried about Stacy I mean since we've been together we were always straight with each other. We'd talked about anything and everything that was going on with us or in the world.

The first time I brought her to my crib she saw all the pictures I took with women a few were cousins but the ones that were in their panties or naked weren't family at all.

I told Stacy Straight up that I was A-Mack. I could still remember her facial expression. Her smile turned me on and her words were unexpected. 'I appreciate you're honesty Stephan there are not too many men being honest these days.'

I let her know that what a true Mack does is be honest. I made a promise to her which was that I'd be there to satisfy her emotionally, financially, and sexually.

I finally reached Eastern Parkway and Troy Ave headed to Albany Projects headed to Stacy's apartment. As I knocked on her door she immediately opened it and jumped into arms.

"It's alright babe I'm here now, so tell me what happened?"

She explained to me what had taken place at Katrina's Parent's house. "Stacy maybe her Parent need more time to forgive you I mean that was their first time seeing you in months."

"But babe if Katrina had forgiven me her parents should have also." Stacy said.

I kissed her letting her know it was alright but it didn't help because she was still crying. I asked her did she forgave herself for doing what she did to Katrina.

Yes! Yes! I have looked Stephan it's been a long night and I love you for being here for me but I'm ready too…"

"Ummm Ohh!"

I was reading her mind and I knew what she wanted. As I licked her earlobe and started kissing her neck her moans were louder than they normally would be.

Stacy couldn't deny it. It was nice having Stephan over she enjoyed his company.

It was the little things that Stephan did that always turned her on and being there for her tonight was no different. Stacy quickly led Stephan to her bedroom.

"Now babe you relax while I take a quick shower." Stacy said.

I knew it was time for me to get into those jeans, but a shower wasn't a problem I mean I love it when a woman keeps herself clean even though we were about to get our freak on.

Ten minutes had passed and Stacy was still in the shower I was becoming impatient.

"Stephan come here please."

Stacy asked me to join her in the shower and as I entered she started washing my entire body with the Zest soap she was using. Soon she made her way legs, then my dick she even washed my feet. 'Man! What a woman.'

As she stood up with water still coming on us she was telling me all the things she loves about me and how much she admires me.

Being the Mack that I was I was used to hearing this kind of talk, but coming from Stacy and looking into her eyes and seeing her facial expression I knew she was telling the truth. She grabbed my manhood pulsating it between her legs. "Wait! Wait! We don't have any protection. I said to her.

"You're right babe because it's still too soon for me to get pregnant."

"Oh really! What are you saying Stacy you don't want to have my babe?"

I asked raising my voice at her.

"Clam down babe all I'm saying is when I have my children I want to be more than someone's baby Mother. I mean I want to be married when I have my children."

'Damn! Stacy was mentioning the M word already to a brother I knew I had to change the subject but she beat me to the punch.'

"Stephan, don't you want to get Married to me someday? She said as she kissed my neck."

I kept silent for a few moments.

"Stephan I'm waiting for an answer." Stacy shouted out.

I was silent again and before I could even say anything she told me she headed to bed and that she'll talk to me later.

"Look I'm sorry babe but you kind of threw me off guard when you mentioned marriage."

Stacy wasn't trying to hear me at all I thought it would be best if I leave because we both had a long night.

As I was heading home I was thinking. Why do most men get shaken when a woman mentions marriage I mean I knew I wasn't wasting her time. I remember my Uncle John saying to me when I was 17.

'Stephan most men just are never ready to be tied down to one woman. Remember want kind of family you come from. We were all Players before we became Mack's and believe me Mack knows when he has the right woman. It all came back to me about what Uncle John said to me before he died of STDs.

I started to remember when my Uncle's sister and my mother would always tell me what kind of women to watch out for. Gold-diggers were the main women my mother and aunt always mentioned to me. 'Stephan always remember a Gold-Digger is like a businesswoman.

They know they don't need to beg a man for shit and they will fuck with you until your bank account goes dry.'

Remembering all of that what my aunt said I had to admit she was right. Because Stacy had never asked for anything it was always me offering to help her out whether it was with a bill which was only two times since we had been seeing each other.

I knew I needed to see someone and that someone was my mother I just had to talk with her about this situation with Stacy wanting to settle down.

The next day after work I was on my way to visit my mother and thinking about what my mom would say if she found out Stacy and I were thinking about marriage.

As I hugged my mom I quickly got to the point. "Stephan I gladly welcome Stacy into our family of all people my son is on the verge of being married. Remember Stephan you will only be the 5th person in our family to get married."

"And who were the ones that got married if you don't mind me asking?" I was very curious about this.

"Well, you know me and your father are married."

"You guys don't count."

"Hush boy and let me finish! My father was married not to my mother but to another woman back when I was a little girl I used to call her a needy wench."

"Wow, Grandpa was married?" I was starting to get excited.

"Stephan let me finish please and don't cut me off again OK now as I said your grandfather was married your great, great, great, great grandfather was married."

"Wait! How do you know all this?"

"Your great-grandmother told me this before she died of cancer and the last two were your great Aunt and Uncle."

After hugging my little brother and kissing my mother goodbye I was ready to go home.

I had a whole different attitude about marriage after hearing what my mother had to say. It's funny how a mother can inspire a son of hers even if he's in his adult life.

As soon as I got home I was ready to talk to Stacy about getting married. I noticed there were 3 messages on the answering machine. My roommate Big Mike had a basketball game so I knew why he didn't answer it.

Message one said... "Stephan this Keisha look I'm calling to let you know I'm coming through tonight and now I'm free so we can do the damn thing on the regular now. I'll be there around seven tonight and you know how we get down so I'll see you when I get there.

Man! I haven't seen Keisha in so long she doesn't even know I'm in a serious relationship.

Keisha was my around-the-way girl before she moved out of the hood which was a good thing, but she left with whom I thought was the wrong guy for her, but that's just my opinion. Anytime Keshia and I weren't satisfied with the sex we were getting from whoever we were dealing with we'd come to each other and talk about it then we'd fuck each other like there was no tomorrow and the positions she loved doing man you'd think she was Samantha from sex and the city. I knew I would have to tell her about Stacy and let her know how serious we were.

I quickly played the 2nd message "Stephan babe I'm sorry for catching an attitude with you earlier, but I meant what I said earlier about not wanting to be a single parent and since you don't work tomorrow I'm going to take tomorrow off.

I'll see you later tonight after I get my hair and I'll make up to you."

'Damn! She'll be here tonight and Keisha's coming here today this is not good.' I said to myself.

Before I could take off my suit and get in the shower the phone started ringing I was hoping it was Keisha.

"Hello!"

"Hey, Stefan it's Kesha I just entered you're building and I'm on my way upstairs so I hope you're ready because I'm going to fuck the shit out of you."

Before I could even say anything she hung up the phone. I met her as soon as

she got off the elevator telling her I wasn't living with my Mother anymore. I let her know I was living with my boy Big Mike. Big Mike was a tall Dark skinned brother whom women adored they loved his height a lot of women found his height sexy. Kesha knew we grew up together. "Well, are you going to let me in or what?"

Hood Lover

I didn't answer her I was too busy looking at her 34d breast. Kesha was looking sexier than I remember. I knew I'd have to let her know about Stacy sooner or later.

"Well hello to you too Stefan you know it's a good thing your brother gave me your number and by the way nice suit." I still didn't say a word to her. I was thinking of how I was going to tell her about Stacy.

What's the matter Stefan you're not happy to see me?" Stacy said as she unbuckled her belt letting her pants fall to the floor.

Kesha, it's not that but I have to tell you I'm in... ummm."

She started kissing my neck and unbuckling my belt and as my paint fell to the floor she quickly took the kisses she was placing on me to my manhood. Kesha grabbed my ass and as she continued sucking and licking all over my balls.

I realized I still hadn't told her about Stacy because a Monagas relationship is not what I wanted out of Stacy.

30 Minutes later Kesha was still putting her lips and tongue to use. Man, this girl had become real good at using her tongue since last I saw her.

"Stefan, are you ready for this pussy now? Because I'm going to tell you now these days I like it rough. I meant what I said earlier about fucking the shit out of you.

Kesha said as she pulled out a condom out of her purse.

I smiled and grabbed one of her legs putting it on my shoulder as I rammed my manhood inside her until it couldn't go any further.

"Ohh... Stefan baby that feels so good go faster."

20 minutes later after I had cum we were at it again this time she was riding me as she kept gyrating her hips.

"Damn Kesha I see you've improved."

She didn't say a word I watched her facial expression as her hips kept shaking.

"Ohhh. Stefan! Ummm… make me cum."

Kesha kept calling my name letting me know how good I was making her feel.

"Doing this every night I'll be going to bed feeling good all the time." Kesha said.

I suddenly heard the door open I knew it was Mike coming from his basketball game. Perfect timing I said to myself because I could tell by Keisha's facial expression she wanted more than just a fuck buddy. I opened my bedroom door giving Mike a pound. I left Kesha in the room to get dressed and told Mike what occurred between me and Kesha I also explained to him what my Mother said earlier.

"Stefan that's nice to hear but, it's time to get high and by the way, I saw you're girl Stacy walking towards the building as I was driving to the parking lot."

"Oh, Shit!" I forgot about Stacy coming here. I quickly spread some Lysol in my room and put on the Iceberg oil I brought from Daniel last week.

"What are you doing that for?" Kesha asked.

"Girl you know I love my room to be smelling fresh."

"Mother, who are you trying to play? I know you've got some next Bitch coming here right?"

"That's the reason why you couldn't give me a straight answer about us right."

Before I could say anything Mike came taping Kesha on the shoulder asking her if would she like to smoke a blunt with him to relieve some of her stress. She told him yes. That's what I loved about Mike even though he was my roommate he always looked out for me in situations like this.

I quickly went to take a shower and told Mike and Kesha I'd holler at them later.

Man life is funny especially relationships even though it was a Complicated relationship between Stacy and me.

They start when the woman is ready and they end when the man is ready to stop doing things for the woman or if he's ready to stop fucking the woman because this was one brother who was going to be devoted to one woman.

9

<u>Stacy</u>

As soon as I reached Rutland Plaza at Building 60 I got on the elevator.

When I got out of the elevator I saw this pretty woman walk out of Stephan's apartment. 'Why the fuck was this bitch coming out of my man's? Oh God please let me be wrong because I swear if this bitch fucked my man I'm going to slap the shit out of him and teach her a lesson as well. Stephan's my man we're supposed to be in a committed relationship. Get a hold of yourself Stacy she anit all that.

I approached her asking why she was coming out of my man's house with a huge smile on her face.

"Oh, you're man Big Mike got some good shit. Next time I'm going to get at least three Dime bags from that Nigga. But I'll give you a little heads up and that's to watch you're back because you're white ass could get yourself hurt out here." Kesha said.

I could see now why she was smiling the bitch was so fucking high she didn't realize I already went into Mike's apartment to see my man. Mike told me Stephan was in the shower and as I waited I suddenly had thoughts of rocking his world.

When Stephan entered his room I welcomed him with a warm kiss.

"Who was that bitch who came out the door? And why did she have such a big smile on her face?" 'I had to be sure that piece of shit wasn't fucking my man.'

Stephane just smiled at me and held me in his arms and started kissing my neck.

"Stephan let go and answer the question who was that bitch coming out of the apartment."

"I don't know babe she and Mike were getting high now I've had a rough day today. Now I'd like to get dressed and relax if you don't mind. Besides, why are you even concerned you're the one I'm in love with."

"And don't you forget it." I said as I threw his towel off and threw him on his bed and started sucking and licking his manhood.

"Oh…That feels good babe."

Stephan started shaking his legs because of the job I was doing.

2 hours later my body was feeling like it was on fire from Stephan sucking my breast and fucking me the way he was, was so good. Stephan came 3 times and I lost count of how many times I came. It had been a while since someone fucked me the way Stephan did. I kissed him on the lips letting him know how good he felt.

"You were good yourself babe and you're pussy was real tight and that's the way I like it." He said whispering in my ear before we dozed off and went to sleep.

One hour later after Stephan got a condom we were at it again. The sex was so intense we both had to take a break and catch our breath.

"Do you see how wet I am?" I said.

"Now it's time to put my tongue to work."

Mmmm "You're a real freak you know that."

"And don't you forget it, I'm a freak for your love babe, and I'm not afraid to let you know I want to be my wife."

I couldn't believe what I just heard. "Stephan tell me you did not just say what every woman dreams of when she is with that special someone?"

"Well don't be silent about the question."

Instead of answering his question, I buried my tongue in his mouth and I went to caressing with his dick trying to get him up again.

"I'll take that as a yes and I could tell you want some more of my good loving."

You better believe I want some more I love you, Stephan. And I'm ready to be your wife." I said before sucking on his neck.

For 90 minutes straight our bodies were moving in rhythm. Each time I came I held Stephan tighter we both had to catch our breath after we finally came at the same time. We both lay there in silence holding each other and fell asleep.

The next morning while I was working I couldn't help but think about the night both Stephan and I shared. I decided to share the news with my girls since I finished my routes earlier. I worked as a Media reader for Con-Edison and these past 5 months changed my life.

Katrina was the first who I called. Her house phone rang about 4 times before her answering machine picked up. "Hello, Katrina it's me Stacy call me when you get the chance girl I've got some news to tell you."

I decided to try her on her cell- phone. "Hello!"

"Hey Katrina, how's it going girl? I've got good news to tell you."

"OK Stacy, but first I'd like to say I'm sorry for the way my parents were acting that day on their anniversary. Now what this big news you have to tell me because I've got news of my own."

"Ok girl you might say it's too soon but Stephan proposed to me," I said with a hugged smile on my face.

"Are you serious girl? That's great congratulations, and Stacy remember don't pay attention to what other people think because you and Stephan are not the only Black and White couple in NYC, and I'm on my way home so if you're in the neighborhood come through."

"Well, that's a good girl because I'm turning down your block now so I'll see you when I get there. "

I'd be lying if I said I wasn't a little nervous but I was.

Shit, it was the first time since the incident with her ex that I was in her apartment.

As I entered Katrina's apartment she quickly ran up on me and hugged me.

"That's a big rock Stephan brought you, girl. You must have really put it on him, girl I'm so happy for you and now let me tell you my good news. I received the letter in the mail yesterday."

"What letter?"

"Well, you guys were going to find out sooner or later. It was my graduate letter for law school I take my next month."

As Katrina showed me the letter we both hugged each other again jumping up and down like little children. "Katrina this calls for a celebration girl let me call Kalaya and Rose."

Rose was the first who we called she didn't answer her cell so I left a message telling her to call my house. We tried her house phone and it rang five times before she picked up the phone.

"Hello!" Rose said in a sleepless voice.

"Girl, it's after 1200pm what are you still sleeping for." Katrina asked.

"Look I'm tired, I didn't get in from the Hospital until 5:30 am."

"Hospital what were you in the Hospital for? Rose woke up and talked to us. I shouted out over the speakerphone."

"What time is it?" Rose said.

"It's ten after twelve." I said.

"I'm woke I'm woke, but I'm still tired. Rose said yearning.

"Now what was that you were saying about being in the Hospital?"

"Alright already, because you two are going to drive me crazy over this phone."

I've been having pains in my stomach and I just threw up before Kenny and I had dinner last night. So my man Kenny being the gentlemen he was drove me to the Hospital after he cleaned up the mess and...."

"And, what girl continued the story what did the doctor say you were sick from what." I asked.

"Damn, you two bitches can be nosy sometimes."

"Katrina and I just looked at each other. "Now Rose we're your girls you know we're just showing concern about you." Katrina said.

"I'm sorry you guys but I'll tell you too what the doctor said and that was I'm 6 weeks pregnant."

"What! Ha...ha...ha..." Katrina and I gave each other a high five and hugged each other after hearing that news. We quickly told Rose our good news and I congratulated her again.

"You go girl." Katrina said.

"What the fuck are you two congratulating me for? I'm not ready for a child what am I going to do.?" Rose asked.

Katrina and I just smiled at each other and told Rose we'd see her in an hour.

One hour later we entered Rose's apartment with smiles on our faces congratulating him. Before we could even hug her Rose started throwing up both Katrina and I jumped out of the way.

"Damn girl, you feeling alright?" Katrina asked.

"Do I fucking look alright bitch? I've been throwing up the last ten minutes."

"Rose you and Kenny will make great parents." I said to her.

"That's the problem now Kenny and I always use protection, so I don't know how the fuck I could be pregnant, and my head feels and my head feels like I was just in a car accident."

Tears started coming down Rose's face I always thought being pregnant was a beautiful thing. Especially when it's with someone you're in love with.

"I've got a fucking career to think about."

"Rose you've got to clean down girl you can't get stressed out."

"How the fuck do you no bitch? You've never felt this kind of pain in your stomach. You anit never been through this shit. Damn it! How the fuck could this happen to me?" Rose shouted out.

Rose, I do know what you're going through because I went through 8 weeks of pregnancy with Darrin's child before I lost it because of a miscarriage. It was from being stressed out all the time. Yes, ladies because of me worrying where he or when that Nigger was coming home.

"What!" Both Rose and I were in shock to hear what Katrina was telling us.

Katrina even explained to us how the Doctor kept her in the Hospital for five days because of house of her depression. "And you won't believe the edit got locked up for drinking and driving."

Soon all three of us were hugging each other like we were children. Katrina suggested that we all go out to dinner tonight just us ladies. I look at Rose she looked like shit and told her she should shower before we go out.

"Bitch you talking I stay smelling fresh and…"

Before Rose could say another word again she threw up in front of us and again we managed to avoid her.

"Man! Rose with your illness maybe you should stay in bed." Katrina said.

No! No! I'm feeling fine I'm still going. Anit no way you bitch's going clubbing without me. Now I'm going out tonight and that's finally. We called Kalaya and I got right to the point of letting her nowhere to meet us.

"Alright, you guy but I'm going to be a little late I've got to see my man before anything."

"I guess she needs some dick to keep a smile on her face." I said to myself.

I quickly dialed Stephan's number letting him know it was lady's night out tonight.

His phone rang 3 times before he picked up.

"Hello."

"Hey, handsome what's up? Look I'm calling to let you know that I'll be out with my girls tonight and we'll be clubbing and all that other shit."

So it's all about you and your girls tonight? That's not what a Nigga needs to hear right now. Right now a nigga needs some pussy so come over babe and please your man.

Tomorrow babe, I already told you it's lady's night out. Now I'll talk with you later.

"Hold on what are you rushing me for?"

I started to think this wasn't a good idea because this Nigga was starting to aggravate me.

"Look, Stephan, you should be happy I called you and let you know what's going on."

"I need to know is it that time of the month for you? Because you sure acting bitchy. Today"

"Stephan that's personal and none of your business and the answer is no. So if I acting bitchy it's because you're acting like a fool."

"Well if I'm going to be your husband it's my business ok White Chocolate and since it's not time of the month for you and since you're not going to break a Nigga off there's something I want you to do for me."

"And what is that if you don't mind me asking."

I what you to close your eyes and picture me tonguing you down, Stacy picture me biting your nipples and sucking your breast. He said sound sexy I've never heard Stephan talk like this. I can't lie, people, he was making me horny.

He continued by saying... "Put two fingers in your pussy and tastes yourself."

"You fucking freak." But I did what he asked over the phone and instead of one, I had two fingers inside myself. And his sexy tone of voice was truing me on.

I started closing my imaginings with Stephan inside of me.

"Hmmm... Hmmm..." I feel you, babe." I said whispering over the phone.

"Imagine that I have five fingers inside you and I'm using my other hand to spread your legs out."

"What five fingers Motherfucker are you crazy? You're a real freak you know that.

My white ass is not letting you put five fingers inside me." I shouted out over the phone.

"Hey, babe my boy Daniel did it with a girl it was his idea, but I'll let you go now just remember I love you."

"I love you too bade. I'll talk to you later. I said as I hung up the phone. I had to admit the heat was picking up over the phone.

As I was ready to leave my house I noticed I had another message on my answering machine. I quickly played it, because I knew it was Stephan with another one of his freaky words so I played it just to hear what he had to say this time.

"Stacy Johnson this is Mr. Marshall I'm sorry to have to tell you this but the Company's... Mr. Marshall paused for a moment. "Well, Stacy the Company's going in another direction. Now Stacy don't take this as being fired take this as being laid off. You can come pick up your next check week."

"Those Mother fuckers!" I shouted out.

I no longer felt like going to meet up with the girls tonight instead I had to think how I was going to pay my bills and how I was going to pay my insurance.

I knew one thing: I had to find another job and finding a job nowadays wasn't easy, especially in New York City.

10

Katrina

I had just gotten out of the shower and this was a night I was looking forward to.

I mean all of us had something to be happy about. I had a lot to be happy about, my new man and the things he would do and say to me. I started fantasizing about Hasson. I spread my legs open playing with myself picturing his basketball fingers were inside of me. I started moving my hips and laughing out loud making me come, babe until my phone rang. "Hello."

It was Stacy telling me she wasn't feeling well and that we should enjoy our lady's night out without her.

"Katrina don't take all night getting dressed girl." Kalaya said.

"Take your time girl because I'm not in a rush at all. Besides I'm still eating this piece of chicken." Rose said.

"Rose that's the baby that's hungry not you, and I'm surprised you're evening having this baby Kenny must have rocked your world, and claimed you as his soul-mate."

"Bitch you don't see no ring on my finger and it doesn't matter if I'm in love or married because you no nobody's calming this ass." Rose said.

"Whatever bitch, but I'm not mad at you. I can't wait until I find my soulmate."

"Wow! Katrina look at you girl." Kalaya said.

Hood Lover

I was still getting ready for our ladies' night out, I already knew who it was and Hasson knew who we were going out. I told him earlier that all of us were going out to celebrate our accomplishments.

When the answering machine came on I heard a familiar voice I'm coming to see you is what we heard.

"Katrina who was that? Because if that's Hasson he sounds terrible over the phone." Kalaya said

"Kalaya believe me that's not Hasson that person just had the wrong number now let's get out of here."

Before I opened the door the doorbell rang and I quickly took a deep breath when I looked through the peephole and saw who it was. "Oh God Kalaya you and Rose should come see who it is."

We were all in shock when we saw who it was.

"Katrina is that who I think it is?" Rose asked.

'Damn! What the fuck is he doing here?'

I was huffing and puffing next to Kalaya and Rose with my arms folded.

"What the fuck is he doing here?" I shouted out just so he could hear me and leave.

"Bitch he's your ex-man, so don't be complaining now you find out what he wants, and don't worry girl we got you back." Kalaya said.

I had no idea what Darrin was at my door for I felt a migraine coming on. Not only was my girls jumping in my face about him but I was mad at myself for the shit Darrin said to me. 'I love you babe but I just got to experience love with other women.

I open the door asking Darrin what the hell he was doing here because this was one piece of ass he was not touching anymore.

Hood Lover

He didn't say a word so I asked again. "Darrin, what are you doing here?" I asked as I locked my door and headed outside with Rose and Kalaya.

"Relax sexy I just came to talk with you. I mean even a Thug needs a lady in his life. And by the way, you look good."

"Darrin what do you want to talk to her about you'd better not ever put your hands on her again or so help me I'll put a bullet up your ass. That's right Nigga I'll be the one to set it off." Kalaya said.

I couldn't believe Kalaya was in Darrin's face like this, but she was dead serious with her words.

Darrin's facial expression changed.

"Bitch do you know who I am? Do you even know what I am? I suggest you get the fuck out of my face for your good."

"Look enough! Don't worry you'll I got this you two go start the car I'll be fine."

I don't know if I was being brave or stupid but I knew I had to handle Darrin because if I didn't he'd just keep thinking I'd let him in my life.

"Katrina have you lost your mind girl don't you remember..."

"Please Kalaya let me handle this, and as I asked before Darrin what the fuck are you doing here?"

He smiled at me saying... "Hello to you too sweet Checks you looking mighty sexy tonight where you and your nosy ass friends off to?"

I swear I was ready to smack fire out of Darrin, but I was not ready to get my clothes messed up. I gave him a vicious look so he'd know I was not fun and games with him. "Darrin number one my name is Katrina and not Sweet Checks. Number two that's none of your business where my friends and I are going. Number three... Ummm!"

Darrin's tongue invaded my mouth. It was the first time someone kissed me other than Hasson. I quickly pushed Darrin off me although Darrin was always a good kisser I

Was loyal to Hasson. 'For you readers out there Hasson was a great kisser there's a big difference.'

I know you felt that sweet cheeks besides I know that new Nigga your with can't use his tongue in both of your mouth's like me. There's no way he's as good as me."

"No Darrin he's great you're not there's a difference."

"Look Darrin for the last time I'm not your woman. I already have a man, a man that loves and cares about me. He's responsible and understanding and most of all he's a man who respects my mind body and soul."

Darrin quickly grabbed my arm having me look him in the eye saying…This is still my pussy and just like every woman you love when I get aggressive and take charge."

My eyes were wide open with amazement. "No, you didn't just try and tell me I'm your property. This anit the same bitch that bailed your ass out of jail on several occasions, this anit the same bitch that would have dinner ready for you while you roam The streets doing God knows what."

"Now I know you don't mean that because you still love me."

I just looked at him shaking my head. "Darrin I've moved on with my life and as far as I'm concerned this conversation is over."

"Don't play yourself sweet cheeks."

Darrin glared at me trying to be Hard-core, but there was nothing he could say.

"Look sweet cheeks let's just put the past behind us and…"

"Look Darrin for the last time my name Katrina. Now I suggest you leave before I call the cops."

"You'll do what?"

"That's right I know your ass doesn't want to go back to jail. Now it's time for you to leave." I shouted out as I let my words sink in.

"This anit over sweet cheeks we still got some things to work out." Darrin said before leaving.

As Darrin continued walking outside I had one last thing to say to him.

Darrin go find some woman to boss around, but be careful about who you fuck with because in this era we're in you have women that are as Ghetto as you men are out here in the hood.

11

Kalaya

Since Katrina came into Rose Truck she's had this angry look on her face. After Rose passed a stop sign I turned to Kiss FM they were playing R-Kelly's song Step and then Trapped in the Closet songs 1-5.

"Is this supposed to make me happy Kalaya?" Katrina asked.

"My bad girl."

I looked at my watch and saw the time it was a little after 6 pm

'Damn,' I thought we missed the drive at five. I looked to see what new CDs Rose had but instead, I found a casket tape that said Bad Boy.

I put it on having no idea what was on this tape. Soon we quickly heard his voice I looked in the mirror and saw it brought a smile to Katrina's face.

It was Michael Baisden I should have known it was him when I saw the title Bad Boy.

"You never stop trying do you Kalaya?"

"Nope!"

"Thanks, girl. It's just that Darrin was the very last person I expected at my door and God knows I don't want him back in my life. I'm already happy with Hasson."

"Ok, you two now hush because I always want quiet when I'm listening to Baisden." Rose said.

"What do you two know about Michael Baisden?" Katrina asked.

Hood Lover

I looked at Katrina like she had just gotten off a bus and just came to make a living in New York City.

"Girl we know all about Michael Baisden. He's always on Kiss FM at 3 pm." I said.

"Ok, you two for the last time be quiet!" Rose said.

We all were ears as we listened to Baisden ask his listeners. "Ok, Kiss family here's the question would you take your ex back if he put his hands on you physically in the past?"

As we listened to the caller whose name was Michelle she said... "I don't know about that one Bad Boy, but my situation is different because my ex he cheated on me with my first Cousin and also my best friend."

"Ohhh!"

"Michael that's nothing because I didn't find out until he was crying in my face telling me how much he loves me and how much he wants this relationship to work."

"So Michelle all the Family wants to know is did you take him back?"

"Yes! And now we are happily married with two children."

"You heard it yourself, Family. Call me at 1877 bad boy."

"I would've never taken that Nigga back if I were her," Katrina stated knowing the same position.

30 Minutes later as we got out of the parking lot heading inside the club the line was very long to get inside. When we finally entered the Knight of Columbus Club on Flatlands. The Hip Hop music was very loud everyone in there had their hands in the air dancing to 50 Cents in the club song.

I suggested to Katrina and Rose we should get our drinks on before we go to the dance floor. Only Katrina and I were going to be drinking Liquor Rose was going to be drinking water because of her pregnancy.

We were all ready to make a toast on our accomplishments in life. I was getting ready to graduate with my BA from Hunter College. Katrina was getting ready for the exam.

Rose already had her BA and a job with a great man who's going to be the father of her child.

"You know ladies let's take it to the head." Rose said.

"Bitch you crazy Katrina and I are drinking Liquor not water like you and this is a long island ice tea we have thank you."

After I made my statement we took our drinks, not to the head but it was close enough. It took me three times to finish my drink my drink the same for Katrina.

One hour later after coming off the dance, we all headed to the bar to relax. I guess after all that dancing all three of us needed a break.

Moments later I was all ears listening to Katrina and Rose talk about the good in loving their men and giving it to them regularly.

"It's time for me to get a man of my own." I said.

"Bitch do you want to look like me because you two don't know caring for this baby around is making me tired. So you two must want to get pregnant."

"Kalaya don't pay Rose no mind girl our time will come to have a child." Katrina said as she and Rose went to the lady's room.

I listened to every word both of them said. I wasn't the type to let people's words go in one ear and out the other. At this point and time in my life, I wasn't trying to put up with the bullshit some men were offering women these days. In my adult life, I never had what Katrina and Rose have which is a real man.

"Excuse me, miss, can I buy you a drink?"

"No thanks!" I said because finding a man in the club for a long-term relationship just wasn't my thing.

"Wait slow down." He said while grabbing my arm and pulling me close to him having me look him in the eye.

"Relax pretty lady and at least let me introduce myself. My name is Michael and I have to let you know you have pretty eyes that go well with your skin."

"Thanks, Mic... Michael." Come on Kalaya get it together.

Michael was a I wasn't the type to get nervous when a man compliments me. As I was walking away I turned to face Michael letting him know my girlfriend was waiting for me. I was one chick this Nigga's game was not working on.

"Wait I never got your name, and do you have a man? Because even when I'm not around you'd picture me tasting those strawberry lips of yours."

I turned to face Michael looking him in the face saying... "No, I don't have a man because I'm tired of dealing with these trifling Nigga's. So what are you about Michael?

"Do you have a woman? Are you married? Do you have any children? Do you have any baby mama drama going on in your life? I'm sick and tired of meeting a man and at the last minute when things are serious, he tells me he's married or he's living with a woman. Michael tell me now I surely don't have time for games."

Rose quickly brought her pregnant overlooking Michael up and down saying…"She sure doesn't have time for games none of us do." Rose shouted out because the music was so loud.

"What's the deal am I being interviewed now?" Michael said with a smile as he shook Katrina and Rose's hand introducing his self."

Michael asked to buy me a drink so I let Katrina and Rose know I'd catch up with them later and that I was going to let Michael drive me home. Although Michael was still strange he seemed like a decent man.

Both Michael and I were on the dance floor getting our groove on especially when the Reggae music came on.

"I've seen love dance before but I've never seen a dance like this."

They were playing Sean Paul's song and every guy in the club was up on a lady in the club. As more songs kept playing and people's music was playing. Michael turned around to face me and quickly kissed me and it wasn't an ordinary kiss. I mean it felt like our tongues were dancing to the music that was playing.

Michael quickly went to kiss on my neck which was one of my weak spots and then tried to insert two fingers inside of me. 'Damn! This brother a real freak.'

"Michael people can see us. I whispered in his ear trying to keep my composure."

"Relax baby nobody can see what I'm doing, especially with my back turned. Now we can take it in the VIP room if you'd like."

"What the…!"

Michael quickly unbuckled my pants and started palming my ass. It took everything I had not to let my pants fall off.

"No! No! This isn't right Michael."

"Relax Kalaya babe."

Michael was now moving his two fingers in and out of my pussy going all around at a very slow pace. It's a good thing people were still dancing because I was becoming very wet and now Michael knew that.

"Ummm." I started biting my lip now as my breathing became heavier and heavier.

"Michael babe not in here, don't make me cum in her please. I said as I slid my hand on top of his."

It's dark in here babe and nobody going to see us now relax because I can feel your body shaking you're ready to cum."

"No! Not in here!" I said as my legs started shaking people in the club must have thought this was some kind of dance I was doing.

Michael quickly whispered in my ear. "Don't worry about getting your panties wet I have tissue in my pocket."

"Uhhh… Uhhh."

Michael quickly kissed me to soften my moaning. I quickly rested my head on his shoulders, because of the heavy breathing I was doing. 'Damn! I must have been one horny bitch to allow this to happen in a club.'

"Michael I can't believe you did that shit! I can't even believe I let you do that what you did I'm ashamed of myself and embarrassed."

As I was walking toward the lady's room I started looking around to see if anyone saw what had just accord but everyone was in their world dancing.

"Damn you Kalaya!" I shouted out.

Don't get me wrong people sure I was looking forward to someone being in love with me.

I mean we all want that in life, but this wasn't the way to go about it. Because of the respect, I had for myself and from what I learned from my past relationships when you sleep with a Nigga on the first night most of the time he loses respect for you.

As I came out of the lady's room finally got myself together.

"Ummm" Michael came kissing up on me I quickly pushed him off of me looking at him and asking… "What are you some kind of Stalker or something? You're not my man."

"But I want to be Kalaya."

Before Mike could even finish a drunk a man walked up to us saying… "Handle your business, Mike."

"Excuse me, motherfucker, I'm not one of his ho's."

Michael just held my hand as we walked outside. "Get off me I can walk on my own besides I don't know you like that. You might have a child I don't know about or even a wife."

Michael quickly started to be quiet I must have figured him out fast.

"Why are you so quiet Michael? You can't answer a simple question, can you? I guess it's almost time for you to report back to your babe mama right?"

And as we walked outside Michael quickly turned his head around saying… "Now that we're outside Kalaya I'm going to tell you this once. "No! I don't have any children. No, I don't have a woman in my life now I can tell you've been hurt in the past, but that had nothing to do with me."

I felt stupid because the look on his face told me he was serious.

"I'm sorry for that outburst. It's just that I'm tired of dealing with losers."

"Babe, believe me, you're dealing with a winner here and let me give you a little advice if you want a soul mate you need to work on your soul."

"And where is this winner taking me? If you don't mind me asking?"

Michael just looked at me smiling. "Kalaya relax there's no need for you to be surprised anymore. So let me take you to a place nice and quiet. It'll be just the two of us trust me."

"Ok! Michael because I'm curious to find out where this place is that you claim is nice and quiet."

"Be quiet sortie and get inside."

Minutes later after getting out of Michael's Nissan Altima, I found myself walking

into his apartment. He quickly took my jacket and I quickly got comfortable making myself at home.

"Take a look around while I roll this joint up."

"Wait! Hold up motherfucker I don't smoke."

"Come Kalaya I know you had weed in your system before."

Michael was right I used to get high back in the day, but that was years ago.

I've changed my life around. I wasn't that teenage girl getting high off of emotions or trying to prove I could hang with certain people.

Once Michael lit his blunt and took a few pulls I happened to notice how funny he started acting.

"You know Kalaya I'm feeling you."

"Nigga who you trying to run the game on? You must think I'm one of those bitch's

in the club that just comes there to find some new dick."

He just stared at me in silence while he took another pull of his joint and inhaled it.

"What are you thinking about Michael? Are you finally willing to confess and admit that you're seriously involved with someone? Or are you going to tell me about you're babe mama drama?"

His face started boiling up I could tell I was aggravating him. But if what I said is true I was going to be out because I was through being that girl on the side for men. "Michael I'm not one of those girls who you can have for the moment and when it's time to build on the relationship you're out the door."

I was waiting to hear what Michael had to say, but instead, he didn't say a word he just stood up and started massaging my shoulders.

Kalaya what you need to do is relax, because I'm going to make your body real hot and sweet. I told you in the club I'm feeling you and I can see already I'm going to be in love with you. I'm going to love the smell of your pussy when my tongue is in it."

Michael kept massaging my neck and shoulders.

"Oh sex me, Daddy!" I shouted out.

Wow! I just realized what I said. I must've caught a contact. I started having visions of Michael's tongue inside me.

Michael laughed at me as he went to put a CD on. I just sat there in silence waiting for Michael to come back in the room he poured a glass of Hennessey for both of us. "Kalaya you sure you don't want some of this joint because it's almost finished."

I was still being silent because I was not going to be getting high with a Nigger I met from the club those days were over.

"Kalaya what are you thinking?"

"Why?"

"Because I want us to be able to communicate together, and why are you being so protective."

"Let's just say it's something we women think about especially when we've been through so much bullshit. And why are you playing an R-Kelly CD I told you I'm not one of those bitches from the club you're used to fucking with."

I quickly caught on to what Michael was saying because the song Sex Me by

R-Kelly came on. I knew it was from his CD 12 play and within seconds Michael was exploring his fingers inside my pussy. It always turns me on when a man knows what he's doing. Michael had his fingers inside me and it was feeling like magic.

Soon his tongue was in my walls and with that sex me song on by R-Kelly I was feeling really good.

"Michael this feels so good and I'm about to cum."

My breathing became heavier and I knew I had to put a stop to this. I knew the difference between love and lust.

"Michael I told you I'm not one of those club hoes you men fuck with."

Relax babe I told you I want to be your lifetime partner." He said unbuttoning my bra and sucking on my left nipple. I could feel his dick rock hard and as he opened the condom he pulled out his pocket took a sip of the Hennessey and rammed his dick right in me.

I let out a loud moan and started kissing him as I bit his bottom lip.

"Mic....." I kept moaning as Michael held my waist tight. Soon Michael had me doggie style and I felt as if I was in another world. My moans were getting louder and louder.

"Slow down babe. Not so rough."

I couldn't believe Michael slowed his pace down. I was feeling better than before going in and out at a slow pace had me feeling good.

"Sorry girl but it's time to speed the pace up."

"Ohhhh!"

"Anit this how you like it Kalaya."

Michael's dick was hitting my G-spot. He kept hitting it repeatedly and as I started Cumming I screamed one hell of a moan that's how good it felt.

My breathing became heavier and before I could catch my breath Michael turned me around kissing my neck and sucking my breast.

"No! No! Michael I don't want to cum again I'm tired.

"What kind of freak are you?"

"One that comes out all night."

"You're a real freak you know that I said as I walked to the bathroom."

As I walked to his bathroom I noticed a tall gentleman come out of his other bedroom. I didn't care who he was because I was feeling good my body was feeling good and I thought Michael might just be the one for me.

"What the fuck is going on out here?"

I couldn't believe what I was seeing Michael was on his knees sucking on this man's penis.

"Michael, what the hell is wrong with you?" Are you one of those men on the DL I hear so much about? Why would you hide your sexuality from me?"

Michael killed the bottle of Hennessey and looked at me smiling.

"Babe I'm in love with you and Frank I was going to tell you but…"

"But nothing Nigga!"

"Bitch you were just something for the moment this is my shit.

"Only I know what this man wants."

"This is insane! You're both crazy." I shouted out I quickly threw my clothes on and headed out the door. Saying to myself it happened again.

Sure I had lost men to other women in the past but never in my life did I lose a man to another man. I was now convinced that even if they reject gay marriage there are still a lot of men on the DL out here in this world.

12

Chris

It was midnight when I arrived home. My feet were killing me walking around at work helping kids and dancing at the Shadow nightclub. I did everything I could think of trying to forget about what Trisha did to me. Leaving to go to Daytona Florida without even letting me know.

Sure some of you may say that's nothing, but I was worried sick about her all week. Any other time she'd let me know where she was and what was going on, but it took a week for her to call me and she was already in Florida.

I mean I'm her man for Goodness sack. Fellas if you've been through this before you know how it is when you're lady's mother is cursing you out asking where her daughter is and you can't answer her because you don't have a clue.

"Chris, can I use your bathroom?" Kim asked.

Kim was a woman whom I met at the club earlier. Now before you readers criticize me and call me all kinds of names just no When Trisha finally called she tried explaining to me that she was in Florida with her friends. Exactly five girls and three guys and I immediately cursed her out.

"It took you fucking ass a whole week to call me and let me know this.

"Just who the fuck are you trying to play?"

After saying that to her I immediately hung up on her ass and got ready for work.

I had all kinds of thoughts going through my mind but only God knew what was going on out there. 'Women always ask why men cheat it's simple because the majority of them allow it, and Trisha was one of them.'

Plenty of times I've tried being the nice guy. Treating women right and treating them with respect like my Mother taught me. But I learned the hard way most of today's women in this era don't appreciate a man's generosity or his kindness.

So again ladies and gentlemen before you go on judging me let me explain why I had to reevaluate my position with some of these women.

Before Trisha and I started dating there was Dorothy. Dorothy was around 5,7 weighed about 135 and had a bagging body.

One day I came to her house on an early Sunday because I decided to go to church with her and before we left I was reading her bible. Dorothy was in the shower and while I was reading I had to come across a letter. I could never forget what I read that day.

'Dear Travis you know what you're doing when it comes to pleases a woman sexually and orally. Sure Chris is good in bed, but you're great just thinking of you and writing this letter is making my panties wet. When I come back to your house I want you to know this pussy's yours, Daddy.'   Signed Dorothy.

I stood in her room in total shock, remembering all the good things I had done for her and her family, especially her daughter. I pulled out my pen and wrote her a quick letter of my own.

Dear Dorothy.

Today was going to be a special day for us. I finally decided to come to church with you only to find out you've been screwing some other dude. I'm sure you've gotten a lot of enjoyment out of it and I'd like to thank you for three things.

1. The education on treating women like yourself like nothing. Women like you are more sneakers than men.

2. Thank you for teaching me everything that shines isn't a diamond because it could be Ford. You know Dorothy I will never understand why you decided to screw another man when you had me for that. But I hope he's working and can support you and you're family like I have. But most of all Dorothy I hope Travis can support and comfort Patricia through these upcoming years like I would have.

3. Dorothy I would love to thank you for creating and giving birth to my new nickname of mine Evil C.   Signed Chris A.K.A Evil C

No   more   Mr.   Nice Guy.

When she came out of the shower I fucked her so hard she started bleeding.

I put Dorothy in every position I could think of just to remind her who ran the show between us. After we were finished fucking that day I told her I'd meet her at Church and left the letter I wrote for her on the wall by her door. I also went to my Church at ST Antony's. Now don't get me, wrong people, I do believe in happily ever after but we're not in that era anymore. I mean a relationship is built on trust and if that trust is damaged like mine was you people will be hesitant to trust or love someone again.

Sure an innocent woman like Kim will be part of my vengeance, but that is what happens when a man gets fed up and decides to reposition his self. Because of women like Trisha and Dorothy, an innocent girl like Kim will suffer.

"Chris, can you help me with this?" Kim asked.

"What is it?" I asked as I stood outside the bathroom.

She opened the door and asked did I had zest soup because the shield soap bothered her skin. "You're lucky because I like you two because I do have zest soap in here. Here you go." I said to her.

She quickly pulled me into the bathroom and threw her tongue into my mouth.

"Hey, what you doing?"

Kim had unbuckled my pants and started stroking me. I could see she was ready to go down on me. I held her head trying to speed up the process.

"Relax Chris and let me take my time I'm the one who's entertaining here."

"Alright be my guest."

You see people this is exactly why I could never make a woman who I met at the club, my wife. Instead of getting to know one another we were underneath the shower head getting busy after I put my rubbers on of curse.

For the next forty-five minutes, we were doing every position possible on our knees. I could easily bend Kim over and give it to her from the back without her saying my back was hurting. That's how flexible Kim was.

As soon as we were washing each other's bodies I looked her in the eye asking... "Kim what's your fantasy I want the truth girl. What can I do to you that no other man has done or let you do?"

She immediately started smiling. "Just for the record I will never lick the crack of anyone's ass so don't ask," I said to her

Well, Chris since you're on the subject. My fantasy is to blindfold and handcuff my man and ride him until I cum at least 3 times. Now tell me yours and as you said to

me about the truth I want the same thing." Kim said as our tongues started dancing in each other's mouths.

Moments later Chris you haven't told me you're fantasy yet.

"Well, my fantasy is quite simple do know what most men's fantasy is?"

"To get their Penis sucked while driving their car."

"No!"

"To have sex in the park?"

"No, no, no Girl! That's me teenage shit."

"To do it in the Movies? Or on the beach? Or give it to his lady from the back with a blunt in his mouth. Yes! That got to be it"

"No! No! No! Girl, don't you know what most men's fantasies are?"

"Wait a threesome?"

"Congratulations Kim you figured it out." I said smiling at her, but I quickly paid the price Kim pushed me on my bed and went straight for my manhood with her lips.

"Chris, where's your phone at?"

I handed her my cell phone and as she dialed the numbers I quickly started sucking her breast.

"Hey, Jane it's Kim I hope I didn't disturb you. Because girl I got news to tell you my man Chris you remember that Brother I must be at the club."

"Wait! Wait! Slow your role. I don't remember telling anyone I was anybody's, man. I already told you I have a girl and if you don't know you know now." I said to her.

"Relax Chris babe. This is girl talk right now and I know we're still getting to know each other. Why don't you get me a glass of water? I mean I am still a guest right?"

I had to admit Kim was right she was still a guest in my house.

As I was headed back into my bedroom I could hear what Kim was saying. I started walking slowly just to hear what she was talking about.

"And bring both of them girl you know how we do. Take the F train to 21 Street Queens Bridge and his address is 21-06 10th Street apt 4a."

" Alright, girl, I'm going to see if he has a Magic stick. Because my man surely hasn't been pleasing me right now."

"Alright, I'll see you in a few." Kim said.

I quickly dropped the bottle of water and cursed this idiot girl out. "Why the fuck are you giving my address to some girl I don't even know. Are you retardate or just plain stupid? And you're talking about being my woman?"

"Relax Chris babe come here don't you want this?"

"Wow!" My eyes lit up. I know Kim was flexible and all but the way she just spread her legs out was amazing. That was something Trisha could never do. No other woman I slept with could spread their legs out like that. I quickly got more rubbers from my draw and I was right back in it.

As I kept giving it to her from the back I grabbed her hair shouting out… "Who's Pussy is this?"

"Owww! Yours Daddy! Yours owww….Chris!"

I started going faster giving it to her harder. "Call me big Daddy and shake your ass girl."

"I am Daddy this pussy's yours."

Forty minutes later Kim was riding my dick like a pro. You would think she took horseback riding at a University or something.

As I kept laying on my back watching Kim do her thing. I heard someone knocking on my door. Who the hell is knocking on my door this late at night? It's after two in the mourning.

" Relax Chris and put your robe on I've got a surprise for you."

Seconds later Kim came back in my bedroom with this fine-ass sister. She looked to be around 5-8 weighing around 155 and had long hair.

"Who the hell is she Kim?"

"Relax Chris and enjoy the show. She's just one of my girlfriends her name China."

Before I could blink they started tongue kissing each other. And as China was taking her close off Kim was shaking her ass in front of me.

"See Daddy this is how us women tighten up the cheeks and that's only if they know how to shake what their momma's gave them."

"Of course I do," China said as they both started doing all kinds of tricks with their ass.

"You ready to do this girl?" Kim asked China.

"Let's do this," China responded.

They both went straight for my manhood. Kim was licking all around the head of m dick, and letting China suck and slurping my balls.

"Damn! Ohh shit!"

It was feeling so good I felt like my eyes were rolling in the back of my head. Damn, this shit feels good. I said to myself.

"Now Chris it's time for us to fulfill your fantasy, and to fulfill mine."

My dick was very hard and as I was putting my rubbers on. Kim was in front of me playing with herself. China went to get something out of her bag.

"Kim lay down and spread them you know what's coming. And as for you, Chris put these handcuffs on. One on your wrist and the other on the bed."

Within moments I was watching China use her tongue on Kim. With her legs spread wide open.

20 Minutes later I watched Kim return the favor to China. 'Damn! What a turn-on!'

Watching two women go down on each other can turn some brothers on.

"Eat this pussy girl! Ohhh…Yeah!" China shouted out.

I watched Kim suck China's pussy very well. 'No wonder she could give good head. These bitches are freaks.'

"I'm ready! Ohhhh, babe. I'm ready Kim."

This was some real entertainment Kim had pre cum all on her tongue and looked at me asking. "Are you ready Daddy?"

"Of course just take my rubbers off."

"No Daddy! I fulfilled you're fantasy now it's time for you to fulfill mine."

Kim got on top of me and put my rock-hard dick inside of her and started riding me. China had her breast in my mouth and started shouting out. "Show this Nigga what good pussy is girl. Ride that Mother fucker girl."

After China did some riding of her own Kim took off the rubbers and started slurping on my manhood. She even started deep-throating it and kept on sucking my manhood. Damn! I know we talked about a threesome but I never expected it to be tense like this.

"Kim! You ready to do the damn thing?" China looked at her then me. Excuse me Chris let me get something out of my bag." China said.

Kim quickly jumped out of bed and grabbed China by the arm saying… "China not him. Not him please?"

"Bitch don't tell me you catching feelings now. You'd better not be catching any kind of feelings. Remember I'm the one who runs shit. You catching feelings for this sorry ass Nigga you can't be serious." China shouted out.

"Hey! What the fuck is going on out there?" I shouted out. Maybe being part of Kim's fantasy wasn't such a good idea.

"Kim let me out of these handcuffs now! This game is over!"

"Wrong Mother Fucker. Because the game hasn't even been gone, but I'll tell you what it's time to play…"

"No China!" Kim paused and asked. "China please stop this nonsense?"

Kim pushed China to the floor looking down at her saying… "China this has to stop. We're not going through with this. Now let's leave from here. Besides I like Chris."

"Bitch what did I tell you?"

Whammm!

China quickly pulled out a 39 and started pointing it toward Kim.

"Bitch didn't I tell you I'm the one who's running shit?"

Before I could blink Kim was shot several times in the chest and there wasn't a damn thing I could do about it.

"Now Bitch! I bet that will teach you who's running shit around here."

"Shut the fuck up you crazy derange bitch."

"What Mother-fucker."

Hood Lover

'Maybe I shouldn't have said that.' I'd better think of something fast.

"China why are you doing this? What is it you want? I'll give you anything Money, a car anything just name it…"

Before I could finish my sentence China had the 39 in my mouth saying… "You want to know what I want I told you it's time to play the game and the game today is riding. I'm going to ride you and if you don't make me cum I'll blow your head off."

I was shaking my head with the gun she had in my mouth.

"Get Hard! Get Hard! Chris come on."

"I'd be lying to you readers if I didn't say I was scared to death but I was.

"Owww! Ohh!"

This Bitch is really crazy I couldn't believe she was riding me with a gun in my mouth.

"Nigga, what the fuck are you a thirty-second man? You can't keep your dick hard? What the fuck did I say if I don't cum?"

China quickly put the gun to my head. "China you don't have to do this. Please, China the Lord is with you."

Shut up Nigga Now tell me where's the cash and I know you have a fucking Jewelry box around here.

I pointed to where it was and told her only I knew where the key was. China quickly took both my Jewelry box and my cash box which was $4,500 I was saving.

"You know Chris it was fun playing the game with you."

"China you're sick I hope you get some help and get that sin out of you. Because I'm sure you've got people that care about you."

"Shut the fuck up Nigger! My parents didn't care about me.

They fucking put me up for adoption when I was only two years of age.

Now you tell me, Chris, what kind of caring is that? Sure I may have a lover here and there but out here in the hood, it's about survival."

"China it doesn't have to be this way like I said there is someone out there that cares about you."

"No one cares about me! You see I only get 20% of whatever is in your cash box. So you see Chris no one cares about me. I can't even get a job out here. This is the type of thing Society wants us to do in this new era. Now, Chris, it's time for you to rest in peace."

Damn it! You one lucky Nigger you know that." She tied my mouth so I couldn't speak and she quickly ran out my door leaving it open. I had never felt so helpless in my entire life. And to make matters worse I had to be at work I a few hours.

Hood Lover

13

Hassan

Katrina and I left my apartment around 7:00 a.m I was heading to work while she was headed to school. I felt great knowing I had a woman who supported me.

As we came out of my building 3 kids came up to me and Katrina. Aron Alice and Allen always came to the after-school programs. When I saw some of the kids whose parents couldn't afford the after-school programs that's when I decided to try and open my on non- profit Recreation Center.

"Mr. Hasson we saw a lady running out of Chris's building screaming call the cops. Murder! Murder call the Cops! And she was grabbing people who were on their way to work including my mommy. Screaming someone's been murdered somebody calls the cops."

"Wait, wait Aron slow down. Now tell me what happened from the beginning and take your time talking this time." I said, but before I could say anything Katrina tapped me on the shoulder pointing towards Chris's building.

"Oh God!"

There were two Police cars in front of Chris's building. I quickly ran towards Chris's building to see what was going on.

As I off the elevator to knock on Chris's door there were several Police Officers in front of his door 5 to be exact. There were people from the City Morg dragging away a body. I knew someone was killed but who; I was hoping it wasn't Chris because I knew he could make women feel like they were Slaut's if they pushed him over the edge.

"Now Mr. Davis you mind telling us your story again and coming to the percent to fill out a police report."

"Chris, what happened here?" I asked.

"Hasson I'm glad you came through Bro. It looks like I won't be coming to work today."

"Mr. Davis answer the question." Officer Green said.

"Look you don't have to answer talk to him in that ton. He's a grown man just like you are." I said to Officer Green.

"Look everyone just clam down let's get to the bottom of this. Shit if I didn't have to work today I'd be home eating some pussy right now Officer Stacy said."

"Now Mr. Davis we found a dead body lying on your bed. We also found you handcuffed to your bed these can be some serious charges against you. So I suggest you start from the top about what happened."

Before Chris could say a word Katrina came up to me saying she saw City Morg people taking a body away and the UPN 9 news was outside.

"Man, this doesn't look good." I said.

"Look, I already explained to you Officers what happened. I had a threesome with Kim and her friend China and when we were in the middle of it both she and her friend China tried to robe me, but instead, China was the one who robed me and Kim…" Chris paused and took a deep breath. "Kim took a bullet and died."

"And you being handcuffed was that part of your threesome? Or did you just handcuff yourself to cover your ass?" Officer Green said.

"Excuse me, Officer, I know Chris well and I know Chris really wouldn't get involved in a situation like this."

"And who are you? Let me see some ID." Officer Stacy asked.

I quickly pulled out my wallet showed him my ID and explained to him the kind of work Chris and I do. They told Chris he'd have to come fill out a Police report at the percent. And come for questioning.

Officer Green quickly read Chris his right and as we got outside the while area was surrounded. A reporter came up to Officer Green and asked him to explain what accord.

"Yes, here you have a case of and the victim Mr. Davis was robed. And because a woman by the name of Kim Williams was found dead he's being taken to the 35th percent for questioning. From the UPN 9 news, this is Mary cold signing off back to you Raymond."

I quickly haled a cab telling him what Percent to go to.

When I got inside the percent Officer Green came up to me telling me how lucky Chris was of not being killed along with Ms. Williams.

"Your friend will be out if the office when the Artists finishes scathing this woman's face because if it's whom I think it is she's wanted for more than murder."

Officer Green said to me.

'These fucking white assholes! Although I didn't necessarily like most of them. Maybe some Police Officers aren't as bad as I heard.'

45 Minutes later Chris and I had finally come out of the percent. He explained to me where he met this girl Kim.

"Hassan I'm telling you, bro, Kim didn't deserve that at all. I promise if I ever see that bitch China again she'll get it from me."

"Chris it's over now! Just let the cops do their job and you know in this era you've got to be careful when you go to these clubs out here."

"That's beyond the point, Hassan. She didn't deserve to die and I could've done 25 to life for something I didn't do."

"That's exactly my point, Chris. You've got to be careful with whom you mess around with especially if it's a chick from the club."

I was hoping that statement would sink in his head but instead, he just gave me a pound and walked toward his building shaking his head.

I didn't want to say anything else because I knew Chris had already been through enough.

As for me, I was headed to work and I knew explaining to our co-workers and to the children that looked up to us wasn't going to be easy.

14

Rose

I had just waken up and got out of my bed. Kenny was doing a double on Ricker's to make up for yesterday when he came with me to the doctor. I was now 7 and a half months pregnant I had just taken a leave of absence two weeks ago and being at home was becoming stressful.

I was ready to make breakfast for me and the baby when I heard my doorbell ring.

"Who is it?" I asked.

I looked through the peep hole and saw who it was. It was Katrina Damn this was a bit of a surprise, and as I opened the door she came storming inside with tears.

"Rose that shit right at all. He didn't deserve that and those children what will they think of him?"

"Him who Katrina? Who are you talking about?" I asked.

I couldn't stand to see people I cared about in tears I quickly handed her a tissue to wipe her tears.

"Now what's going on? Did Hassan hurt you already? I'm tired of you crying

Over these men, if they don't want you the Hell with them. I was so used to Kalaya always crying over men and now Katrina was too."

"Rose you're got the situation all wrong. I told you people Hassan's a great man. It's his friend Chris you remember the one I was going to hook Kalaya with."

"Owch! Owww!"

"Rose you, alright girl?"

"Don't pay me know mind girl. It's just the baby kicking."

As I sat on the couch Katrina explained to me what happened with Chris. She told me everything Hasson told when he called her on her cell phone.

"The Mother fucker shouldn't have known better. You only use handcuffs with your partner."

"Rose this isn't funny. What if Chris loses his job for this shit? Hasson would be torn up with that."

"Look Katrina just calm down. What I said wasn't meant to be a joke. But you've got to admit the Nigga was thinking with his big head and not the head where the brain is at. But it's like I always said some Nigga's dick's don't have a conscious."

I suddenly felt a migraine coming on to me. I had to make sure I wasn't getting stressed over this bullshit. I quickly changed the subject.

You know Katrina I wish men went through this kind of pain we go through especially the physical part."

She looked at me as if she didn't have a clue as to what I was talking about.

Being pregnant can be stressful! Nigger's don't know what it's like to go through 9 months of this shit."

"I don't either."

"Oh, you will bitch trust me you next."

Katrina looked at me as if I was joking not that I didn't mind being pregnant but on certain day I felt real tired and miserable. Before I could go on the doorbell rang again.

"Now what! Who the fuck is it?" I shouted out.

As I opened the door he smiled at me with excitement. I smiled back and quickly made my smile disappear.

"Wow! Rose look at you."

"Yeah Travis it's been a long time and this isn't a good time for you to be around me. So it'll be best if you leave."

"Damn Rose! You don't have to be so cold to the brother." Katrina said.

"Whatever!" I said as I walked back into my living room to lie down.

"So Travis what's been up with you?" Katrina asked.

Well for starters I've been with Con Edison for a while now. But that's not what I'm over here for. I came to ask Rose a big question."

"Oww Please! Travis! Haven't we been through this already and don't you see how the fuck I look now? I'm pregnant."

He looked at me in frustrating.

Rose, I remember what we discussed. Look I didn't come over here to fight or argue with you. I came to see my friend who's like a sister to me.

'I was great to hear him say that.'

"I also came over because I needed a good listener. My girlfriend and I are engaged but her parents and relatives don't like me because we've broken up before they don't think it'll work out. Isn't that ridiculous?"

"Well, why did you two break up in the first place? Katrina asked.

'I was curious to know the real reason myself because this was one relationship Travis never talked about.'

"Well, ladies just like there's several reasons why I loved her there were several reasons why I broke up with her at the time. At the time she wasn't supportive, she had lost her feelings for me but still wanted me around her."What is that bitch crazy? I asked.

The list goes on Rose. She started disrespecting me. Having guys call her house and ask me to be quiet. I mean you can get angry with me if you want to but I just couldn't take it anymore. I started feeling like I was ready to kill someone. I mean I was busting my ass trying to find a work at the time and always looking out for her. Once I noticed how much she lost it.

I had to leave her Rose you and Katrina and the people reading this have got to understand I felt like I was going to kill someone.

"I'm sorry to hear that Travis." Katrina said.

"It's alright because were back together and we're engaged."

Travis went on to tell us all the restaurants he and his finance have been too. I couldn't believe a wave of jealousy hit me. I felt like screaming at him. I felt like screaming at him. How could he take the back doesn't he realize she's going to disrespect him more?

I looked at Travis shaking my head and Katrina looked at him.

"Travis my family isn't happy with the man I'm with. But you can't let that ruin your relationship. I've learned some family members are just unable to let their family members experience true happiness."

You know Katrina you're right. Her parents and everyone else didn't find out we were back together until we announced our engagement. So when we first got back together wed kept it on the down low."

I was still curious and skeptical about Travis and his fiance.

"Travis, how exactly did she feel? I mean what did she say when you two got engaged?"

"Well, Rose she told me her body what's me so much. For what I miss at home and no one has to know about us. So let's keep this on the down low."

"I hear that!" Katrina said.

Travis quickly came and kissed us on the cheek. Thanking us both for listening to him. I might have felt a little wave of jealously but I was happy for Travis. He was always one of those people looking for love and he was finally blessed with a Soul-Mate.

Later that evening after Katrina left had insisted that I let him cook dinner.

I agreed and he headed into the kitchen to get started.

"That's right babe treat me like a Queen." I said as Kenny served me my plate with a smile.

I was on the verge of what most sisters would call a perfect life. A great job with the Government, a well intelligent and strong black man whom I was having a baby with.

Life is good when things are going your way. After we finished having dinner Kenny quickly came and took my plate and then led me to the bed room. His soft lips gently touched mine, and if you readers didn't catch on yet. Kenny leading me into the bedroom meant it was time for some serious love making

15
Katrina

The alarm buzzed at 6:00 a.m. I quickly reached over and turned it off and called Hassan to see how things went with Chris.

"Hello." Hassan said in a sleepless voice.

"Good morning babe. How did things go with Chris?"

"Well, the good news is he hasn't been charged with a crime. The bad news is he may have to go to trial."

"What?"

"Look I've had a long night, don't you have a graduation I had forgotten about it."

"It's only Wednesday Hassan. But I do have to get ready for work."

"Same here, but before you leave why don't you picture me holding you with my arms around your waists and my tongue inside your walls."

I kept silent for a moment and started picturing Hassan using his long tongue in all the right ways.

"Katrina you alright girl?"

"Oh, Hassan! Yes! Yes, I 'm just fine." I smiled because only you ladies reading this would know how it feels when your man knows how to use his tongue in different ways.

Two days had pasted and it was now time for me to graduate.

Both Hassan and I pulled in a Lincoln Limo. Everyone was there to watch me get my degree. I had one filled with family members and the other with friends.

When the graduation was over my boss came up to me and congratulated me. He even congratulated me for passing my bar exam which I haven't even taken yet, but that's the kind of confidence Mr. Snow had in me.

"Katrina here's a picture of your new office. I'd like to hire you fulltime. I think you've earned the right to be a full-time lawyer now."

Hassan quickly put his tongue in my mouth congratulating me. My father got in between us and started hugging me. 'When was he going to realize I wasn't his little girl anymore?'

"Wait Daddy I haven't even given him an answer yet."

My father looked at me asking... Katrina, aren't you going to accept his offer? I mean you'll be a lawyer fulltime now. You see Mr. Hassan this is why I didn't want anyone screwing up my daughter's life."

"Daddy this isn't the time or place for this!" I shouted out.

"Damn, can't you two act like civilized people for a change? I mean I just graduated College. Does that mean anything to you to you guys besides arguing?"

My dad can be such a jerk sometimes but Hassan is one of those brothers that can keep his emotions in check. Now, ladies, you've got to love a man like that.

After everyone calmed down I kissed my Mother and Father. I could tell they were proud of me for going back to school and finally apologized to me and Hassan for the commit he made earlier. He even shook Hassan's hand which was a surprise.

"It's all good Mr. Hill I just hope you realize now I'm in love with your daughter. And I'm going to support her just like she supports me."

This was a lovely thing to see my father and Hassan finally able to look at one another and smile at one another.

30 Minutes later my boss took me to see my new office in person. I quickly started looking at it and seeing how huge it was I sat back in

my leather chair letting Mr. Wilson know I accepted his offer. I quickly called my Mother letting them know I accepted Mr. Wilson's offer.

"That's very nice honey. Both me and you're mom are very proud of you. And I want you to know honey although I may still have doubts about your boyfriend Hassan seems like a real nice guy."

"Thanks, daddy. Coming from you dad that's a compliment I'm sure Hassan would love to hear that. And keep my cap and gown clean dad."

After I got off the phone with my dad I heard out of the office with Mr. Wilson.

"Mr. Wilson let me get a fresh start on Monday. Because you better believe this young lady is going to be the best damn lawyer she can be."

That's nice Katrina see you Monday." Mr. Wilson said as he drove off in his Lincoln Navigator.

"Katrina! Katrina!"

I knew that voice and as I looked back before I got in the back before I got in the train station at Borough Hall. Both Hassan and Chris came out of a cab. It was a good thing my boss went home he might have thought these two were a bunch of stalkers.

"What are you two doing here?"

Hassan's lips quickly met mine.

"What's all that about?"

"Babe I accepted Mr. Wilson's offer."

"That's great babe. Because Chris has something he'd like to talk to you about."

"What do you finally want me to hook you and Kalaya up?"

"That's nice Katrina, but this hear is far more important. Remember when I said I may have a trail."

"Yeah! So who's representing you?"

"Chris don't tell me you were thinking of representing yourself? Because you'd have to be a Chameleon to do that."

"Very funny Katrina, But seriously I know this might be asking a lot. But I'd like for you to represent me."

"What?" I quickly put the smile I had on my face to rest. I could tell Chris wasn't kidding at all about this. Hassan suggested that we have dinner and talk about this.

I quickly called Kalaya on her cell phone and told her to meet us at Juniors in an hour.

45 minutes While we sat down getting comfortable and looking at what was on the menu Chris gave Hassan and Kalaya a serious look.

"Katrina I'd like for you to represent me, because if I have to go to trial. I want a lawyer who I trust. As I said before I know I'm asking a lot but take your time thinking about it while you're at home tonight."

I kept silent for a moment for the first time I started questioning my new Profession.

As we were all having dinner I was still thinking about Chris's case. Sure I believed he was innocent and all but this would be my very first case I'd be representing my man's best friend, And.

"Katrina."

"Katrina! Are you all right?"

"Oh! Sorry babe. I must have been day dreaming."

Hassan quickly stood over me and then got on one knee.

"Oh my God! I don't believe this."

I quickly felt my heart beating faster than a normal heart.

"Katrina again I'd like to congratulate you on graduating and now you're working in a law firm full time not many people get that opportunity. I'd like you to know how much I respect and appreciate you being in my life."

"Hassan I...I love you." My breathing became heavier than before and I was becoming nervous by the second.

"Hassan, what are you doing?"

"Relax my love because there will never be a day, you'll ever hear me say that I want and need you out of my life. Babe, I want to spend as many decades as we can together. And I don't know what lies in my future, but I know I'd like you to be part of it.

"That's why I'm asking you Katrina Hill to marry me?"

I turned around and saw all eyes were on us.

"You go, girl!" Kalaya said.

"Kalaya I haven't even given the man an answer yet. I mean this is happening too fast."

"You haven't given the man an answer." Chris said with a smile.

"I kept trying to catch my breath. Yes! ...Yes! Hassan, I'll marry you I can't wait to be your wife. And yes Chris I'll represent you."

Everyone in the restaurant including the people working there was clapping and showing their support and Hassan's engagement.

We all started walking towards Park Slop and as we were walking I asked Chris to tell me everything the night Kim Williams was killed.

"Well as I told the Police I met Kim at a club and we were both drinking and telling each other our fantasy. She asked me to come to my house and of course, I said yes."

"Just like every other Brother out here quick to bring a female you meet from the club to your place just to get some..."

Look Trisha and I were having problems at the time. Sure I was going to take anger out on Kim and fuck the shit out of her, But that was all I had on my mind nothing but sex."

"Then how did this other woman get involved?" Kalaya asked.

"She called her over after we talked about each other's fantasies, and since hers was fucking a man while he was in handcuffs and mine was a threesome. I guess you could say we both full filled each other's fantasy."

"That still doesn't tell me how she ended up dead." I said.

"Well, Kim and her girlfriend China planned on doing this with someone. It just so happens that I was the victim last night. Kim even started catching feelings for me and that drove China crazy."

I was quickly putting two and two together China got jealous and shit Kim while Chris was still handcuffed. And there wasn't a damn thing he could do about it.

By the time we got to Flatbush and Bergen, I kissed my fiancée goodnight and told him and Chris Kalaya and I were going out to celebrate my graduation.

Chris walked up to me thanking me again. "I'm going to do my best to prove your innocence, Chris. You and Hassan enjoy the night."

Kalaya handed Chris a piece of paper. "You know Kalaya if you weren't Katrina's girlfriend I'd think you were a Gold digger."

Kalaya quickly snapped at Chris. "Excuse me! Nigger that's something you would be thinking wrong. I am an educated black woman and if your ass wasn't busy sticking everything out here you would know my graduation is next week."

"Kalaya!"

"I'm sorry Katrina and Hassan but I will not have any Mother fucker disrespect me."

"Hold on no need to get upset I was only kidding Kalaya That's what's wrong with you women you're all too emotional. All I was trying to say was now that I've gotten to know you I can tell you're not the materialistic type."

"And you'd better remember that."

Hassan and I looked at them both. I knew Kalaya was ready to start swinging on Chris but I quickly grabbed her by the arm telling her let's leave.

"Kalaya girl we've got to celebrate our graduation even though yours is next weekend." I said to Kalaya.

"Sounds good girl but I just wish Rose and Stacy could be here. You know it's a good thing you're going to represent Chris. Lord knows he needs it and Lord knows I was ready to knock some sense into him earlier."

Kalaya was wearing a tight low-cut red Sean John dress with her hair and nails done. I was wearing a black low-cut Sean John dress.

After we got out of the cab it seemed all eyes were on us we entered the Sin city strip club.

Katrina look at this place it's all a bunch of Nigga's up in here. There are very few ladies up in her except on stage and that's what I'm talking about. Let' say just hope there is not a shootout before the night is over. Kalaya said.

"Your right Kalaya we should be leaving now."

"Wait! Katrina we just got here besides the night is still young. Wow, look at that brother dancing up on stage come Katrina let's get a closer look."

"Hello, Ladies! Congratulations on your engagement Katrina by the way where's your man at?"

My face quickly started boiling up this is the reason why I wanted to get out of here and go somewhere else.

"Darrin, what the hell do you want? Because God knows I didn't want you back in my life. Look why don't you just find yourself a new girlfriend."

"I have one now. She's coming back with our drinks now I know you're not married yet and I know you wouldn't mind me fucking you in every way possible including upside down."

"Excuse me Nigga have you lost your mind."

I threw my fists up like I was ready to knock the shit out of him, but I quickly had a flash back about the last time I did that.

"Be careful cousin that's my man you're attempting to swing on."

I couldn't believe what I was hearing. My cousin Valerie was here dating my ex. I became curious as to why she would choose Darrin to be her man.

"When the fuck did you two start seeing each other?" I asked.

I didn't care if certain people in the club thought I was making a fool of myself.

"Valerie don't you know dangerous Darrin is? Aren't you aware of the stress he'll put you through?"

"She right Darrin, if you hurt her cousin in any kind of way I'll kill your ass, you fake ass pimp."

Darrin looked at me and Katrina and took a sip of his drink. Darrin had his hands all over my cousin telling me they met on Myspace.

"Darrin and I have fallen in love and this is by far the best relationship I've been in my hole adult life. And my man gives me great loving so you tell me cousin what does that have to do with stress?"

"You tell her babe. Katrina Valerie was even at my Mother's funeral something you could never do. I remember when it was my uncle's funeral you claimed you were too scared. Now instead of you two ladies worrying about us and our relationship. You two need to pay attention to who's coming to the stage next because if I'm not mistaken you two will be surprised." Darrin said as he took another sip of his drink.

Both Kalaya and I couldn't believe what we were seeing. We both looked at each other in shock. Both of our mouths were wide open.

"So this is the reason she hasn't been in touch with us." Kalaya said.

The M.C. announcer quickly yelled out. "Show your love for White Chocolate.

Both of us were surprised as we watched them shake what her mama gave her in front of all these horny men.

16

Stacy

I had the entire club looking at me doing my thing. I was told to always smile and make eye contact while on stage. Since Brain A.K.A Babe Cream came he's made me comfortable. He always said to me 'Make the men, especially the Married ones, make them go home with something to think about.'

The more dollars that were thrown on stage the more I kept eye contact with the men that were there. The DJ quickly threw on Sean Paul's song.

I tried my best to just concentrate on the music and just dance, but I heard one of the men yell out... "Turn around and show us their cheeks."

I kept dancing and wounding my hips and quickly turned around giving these Niggas in here a taste of hear well, ok great I can shake my ass.

As the style of music changed so did my dancing I started moving at a slow pace.

Because the song that was playing now was sex me by R. Kelly. I kept dipping and turning as well as claiming and sliding down the pole and still being able to keep eye contact with the crowd.

All you heard was men hollering. I knew there were some jealous females backstage but I didn't give a fuck. And God knows I didn't give a flying fuck about these people in here. They don't understand or even care about my struggles because in this business it's all about the Benjamins.

I started pointing fingers at men in the crowd. Quickly catching their imagination and as these sex fens kept throwing 1'$ 10'$ 20'$ 50$ one man even threw a $1000 bill. You would think I made him cum in his pants, but I knew he was too drunk to realize how much he put out there on stage. There were so many bills on stage when the song was over I needed Babe's Cream to help these bills off stage.

I felt as though I brought the dog out of every man that was in the club, although other ladies were going on stage I knew my juices were the ones men wanted to taste. Ever woman in the club weather they were on stage dancing or just on the floor giving lap dances and serving drinks. Every woman had their reason to work at Sin City club. Now, people, before you go on and judge me you'll have to understand I needed money. After I had lost my job, my man, Stephan had proposed to me that same night. Although I accepted the proposal I knew I needed money not just for our wedding, but for my bills as well. I guess you can call it Pride as to why I didn't tell Stephan or anyone else about me losing my job. For weeks I was all over New York City looking for work.

I was always spending money, faxing my resume or e-mailing it. Interview after interview I still wasn't getting any call backs sayings I was hired. It had become so frustrating I even thought about hanging on the street corner and making fast money like everyone else. But I was determined to make money the legal way and not let the streets get the best of me.

I spent almost three months looking for work so I could pay my bills like my rent, car insurance, and car note not to mention my phone bill and my groceries.

I found an eviction notice on my door saying I had 30 days to pay my rent. I was already three months behind and the day I tried taking out a loan was the day my life changed. Brain who I knew as a School Safety Security guard at high school just happened to be there. I asked him if he was still working at Tilden and he started laughing at me.

He told me he started his own business and I started laughing because here was a gentleman mixed with a Pit Bull. He had 95% of the women and female students wanting to get in his jeans. And the other 5% of female students and Teachers that were wanting to suck him off. Either they were married or too nervous to tell him what was on their minds which I couldn't blame them, because my panties were getting wet just by looking at Brain. After we both handled our business I explained to Brain about the rejection the bank just gave me. I even told him why I needed the money he offered me a lob at his company and invited me to his place for dinner.

As we drove towards his place over on Linden Blvd I was telling him what I did after High School and how I was going to be a married woman soon and he congratulated me. When we entered his apartment I complimented him on how net his place was looking. Brain quickly went to put his new CD which was R- Kelly's trapped in the closet. I remember it so well because what I did to him you readers would've thought I was one of those crazy deranged women. Brain asked me if I could dance in front of him and I immediately grabbed his pubic hair and started screaming out.

"Nigger I'm not one of these fucking chicken heads you be fucking out here in the world."

Brain pushed me off of him knocking me to the floor and telling me to calm down Brain had asked me again to dance with him this time putting R Kelly's Chocolate factory and the song that was playing was Step.

As the song came on I slowly started moving my hips. I swear on everything I love once I saw Brain smiling I quickly threw my shorts and Bra off and bent over jiggling my breast in his face. Brain playfully pinched my left nipple and licked my other. As he was whispering to me how beautiful I was and that I should be a stripper.

"For what it's not like a brother like you can handle my juices anyway, and I want to know are the rumors true?"

"What rumors are you talking about?"

I explained to him it's something we females talk about when we're in a situation like this. 'Now ladies we all know good girls don't tell right.' Besides I was only engaged not married.

After Brain mentioned a stripper I unbuckled my belt and paints and bent over.

Brain's eyes we're wide open and after putting in me from behind. I let out a very loud moan and started screaming at him. 'Give it to me Daddy!'

After throwing my pussy on Brain we collapsed on his bed. He explained to me how he could help me.

I wasn't shocked anymore when Brain told me he was the owner of the Sin City club. He told me the kind of money I could make there. I accepted his offer because I needed the money and since then my life has changed grammatically.

As I walked out of the locker room and headed out of the club both my arms were grabbed. "Wait, Stacy! What in the world are you doing here? You can't lie to us we saw you on stage not too long ago." Katrina said.

As I turned around I saw that it was Katrina and Kalaya. Just great I said to myself. I knew people that were close to me would find out but not like this.

"Look you'll don't understand. I needed the money to survive out here most people don't understand when you get fired from a job you have to do what's necessary to survive and I don't mean sell drugs."

"You're right! But have you forgotten you have friends? For God's sake Stacy we would've helped you, but we see why you haven't been in touch with us." Kalaya said.

"Does Stephan know about this?" Katrina asked.

I gave them both a look telling them both I didn't want anyone else including Stephan to know about this. It's not like I was one of those Strippers having all kinds of Nigger's run there dicks and tongue's all up in my pussy. I was just on stage working I mean it's a job for damn sake.

"Look let's just get out of here." I said.

"But who's that sexy ass brother in thongs? How freaky is he?" Kalaya asked.

I told them both that it was Baby Cream and that he was the owner of the Club. As we made our exit from the club we went into my brandnew 2005 Escalade. I explained to them I had brought it two weeks ago.

"I hope you can keep up the payment on that car note. But seriously Stacy are you sure this is for you?" Katrina asked.

"Yeah!" I answered.

"I mean are you positive you want to do this?" Katrina asked again to see if I was confident about this.

"Yes!" I shouted out. 'I mean who these bitches think they were questioning my motives.

"Be easy Stacy! But do your girls remember." Kalaya said.

"I'm sorry but you don't understand this is something I have to do. I almost got kicked out of my apartment but everything's alright now besides Brain's made this job very comfortable for me. I just give him half of what I make each night."

"What?" Kalaya said.

They both gave me a weird look. "Look you two there were no jobs out there that wanted me so I just had to look at other opportunities." I said as I put my Escalade in drive.

"Why didn't you just go to Stephan or one of use if you needed help? Can't you see this Nigga's pimping you?" Katrina said.

Excuse me? Look you two I take care of myself. You guys know my family and I don't keep in touch. As for my girls and my man just like him you'll we've been able to help me for only a week or two. Eventually, you'll would've been tired of helping my white ass. With the money I make Brain sees that I'm able to take care of myself and still save up for my wedding. Can't you two see this is a positive thing it maybe a hustle here and there but…"

They both touched my shoulder telling me to relax. "Stacy we're you're girls you know we've got you're back. I understand now why you missed my graduation." Katrina said.

"And you better not miss mine bitch you here me! Now tell about this Brain dude because the way he was looking at you on that stage I know you put it on him."

"Kalaya its just business strictly business now drop it."

"Whatever bitch! We aren't stupid I just pray you find the courage to tell Stephan." Katrina said.

After driving both Kalaya and Katrina home I headed for Stephan's place. Although Kalaya and Katrina had given me a lot to think about this was one thing off my chest, because Stephan is the type of brother that every woman dreams about so I knew I had to approach him right about this.

"Damn!" I shouted out.

As I drove down Rochester avenue I kept thinking about how was I going to explain this to Stephan and how should I approach him because this wasn't going to be easy.

After finding a parking spot I walked toward Rutland houses I was let in by one of their security guards.

"Where you going, miss?"

"Excuse me?"

"I'm sorry but you look like you need some inspiration in your life."

"Thank you! But I can get my inspiration from my God and my man."

I exhaled before I even knocked on Stephan's door. Explaining this too Stephan isn't going to be easy I kept repeating to myself.

After knocking on his door he quickly let me inside welcoming me with a kiss. "That feels good baby," I said as his soft lips made their way to my neck.

I gave Stephan another kiss as we both started unzipping each other's pants. My hands were all over his dick as I got down on my knees as I started licking the head of it.

"Relax baby. Let's take this in my room before Big Mike comes out of the shower."

"You're right besides I need to talk with you."

"Later baby."

Stephan went back to kissing my neck as he took my short and bra off.

"Stephan… Stephan…" I kept moaning as he started sucking my nipples and then my neck and then sucking on my bottom lip."

Baby we finally finished making our project. Our CD label should be released soon. Damn! I'm blessed. I'll be married so plus we've got our CD label coming out."

"Stacy you ok baby?"

"Yes, I'm alright." Only God knew I lied. I quickly look in Stephan's eyes as I started sucking his manhood. "That' it girl because with me in the music industry, I think you'll make a great house wife and…"

I snapped at him immediately. "And you'd be thinking wrong!" Who did this Nigger think I was? Sure we were engaged but me being a house wife wasn't something to think about.

"Hold up baby! No need to get angry. I wouldn't want our night going bad or anything so just relax."

"I am relaxed I just don't want to have a failed marriage like others out here today."

"Are you convinced out relationship is going to fail?"

I kept silent. I wanted to tell him so badly what I've been doing.

"Stacy, are you scared? Come on answer me because if you've even thought our marriage will fail then it will."

I quickly responded letting him know I wanted us to get married and how much I wanted it to work. "I want us to be together forever."

"Then stop tripping we're both saving for this wedding. We're both working and we both love getting buck wild with each other.

"You're right." I admitted.

I climbed on top of Stephan right after he put his rubbers on. Stephan grabbed my waists and then palmed my fat white ass.

35 Minutes later Stephan had my ass cheeks spread wide open. His dick felt so good hitting my womanhood from the back I started biting his pillow.

"Faster, faster this shit feels good." I shouted out.

Before the night was over I sucked his dick one more time and told him how much I trust him we were starting to understand each other.

I finally started to fall asleep in his arms, but I still hadn't told him about my stripping and the money I was making. Shit, I didn't even tell him I had sex with Brain. I Could picture Katrina, and Kalaya, saying 'Girl you'd better get you're shit together

17

Chris

Ladies and gentlemen of the Jury for the next few weeks you all will have a lot of very disturbing evidence. We intend to show that the defendant sitting at the other side over there Chris Williams killed Kim Johnson. You will all hear testimony from witnesses to one of the most ingénues crimes of our time. We are all hear to witness justice sure the defendant was arrested but that's not justice and…"

"Objection your honor she's harassing the defendant." Katrina said.

"Objection overruled continue." Judge Powell said.

"Thank you, your honor. The prosecution will no doubt prove that Chris Williams killed Ms. Johnson with a weapon everyone nowadays has a gun. I mean it's the easiest way to win a fight or argument."

"Objection your honor this case is not about weapons on the street nor has my client been charged with any kind of weaponry."

"Objection sustained there will be no harassing here in my courtroom."

"Sorry, your honor but I'm sure most of you all here are tired of people getting shot at in this world. Sure we have killings overseas and our people fighting a war they know nothing about. But in this courtroom today I will do my best to see that justice is served."

I sat there and watched Gwen Goods do her thing. In this case, I was her victim you see people Gwen and I went on a few dates back when Trisha and I first started seeing each other. To make a long story short I stopped calling her after I got in those jeans during our third date. I started feeling as if I was in a no/win situation. Gwen had everyone's eyes on her in the courtroom. She had on a red two-piece suit. I'm sure the men in here were taking a good look at Gwen's sexy legs including the Judge. The Judge was a black man who looked to be in his middle fifth ties.

"Ms. Goods call your first witness to the stand."

"Yes, your honor. My first witness is Officer Green."

'Just great.' Damn Those Cops.

"Mr. Green, what did the defendant tell you and you're partner when you arrived at his apartment?"

"His exact words were he had a Manajatwa with two ladies."

"And one of these ladies was Kim Williams am I right?"

"Yes! Yes, you are." Officer Green said.

"Now Mr. Green you told news reporters that you and your partner found Mr. Davis in handcuffs. Is that true and what was your reaction to it?"

"Yes! It's true but my reaction was to get to the bottom of the crime. Because you have people getting killed left to right out here and 65% of it is by a person getting shot."

"Mr. Green did you and you're partner arrest Mr. Davis because you felt that he murdered the victim Kim Williams?"

"No Mr. Davis was arrested and brought to the 19th   Percent for questioning but before we arrested him I did ask him did he kill her and handcuffed himself to his bed to cover his butt."

"Nigger I told you're dumb as partner me, Kim, and China had a threesome! It just so happens that me being handcuffed was part of it! Don't you ass know the freaks come out at night?" I shouted out.

"Mr. Davis I will not have that N-word in my court room nor will I allow another outburst like that because I will have you removed from this court room and removed from prison. Remember I have the power to do it too." The Judge said.

Just great another Blackman who's made it big and thinks he can do anything. I could see how this was turning out I was straight-up guilty until proven innocent.

"Ms. Goods ask your next question. And this time stick to the facts and not someone's opinion." The judge said.

"So Mr. Green Mr. Davis was handcuffed when you and your partner arrived right?"

"Right."

"How did he say she died and how did he kill her?"

"Objection your honor there is no evidence my client killed anyone." Katrina said.

"Sustained."

"Mr. Davis told us that her partner shot her and then robbed him. I told my partner to look for clues while I questioned the defendant."

"Yes."

"One more question Officer Green did the defendant say anything else to you."

"Yes, he kept repeating that the victim Kim Williams did not deserve this."

Thank you for know further questions you honor but I would like to say something to the ladies and gentlemen of the jury in here and those in the courtroom as well. Because when someone dies at the hands of another we all know that is called murder. And we are here to prove that the defendant committed murder. Sure the defense will try to prove he's innocent but…"

"Your honor!" Katrina said.

"Ms. Goods get to the point you're trying to make."

"Ok! Your honor my point is Justice must be served. Here in this courtroom, Gwen said as she walked back to her chair.

"You may cross-examine."

"Thank you, you're honor. Mr. Green tell me if I'm right or wrong but didn't my defendant cooperate with you and you're partner? And didn't my defendant answer you're questioned at the 19th percent right before he filed out a police report about him being robbed?"

"Yes."

"So in detail Mr. Green what did my Client feel out in the police report?"

"Well, he said how it was a setup, and how he was robe."

"In the police report did he describe who it was who killed Kim Williams and who robbed him?"

"Not in so many words, but he said it was a female in her late twenty's."

"Did my Client give a name?"

"Yes, he said her name was China."

"Thank you, no further questions, your honor."

The Judge looked at Gwen for about 15 seconds before she called her next witness.

Everyone in the courtroom knew you had to be strong to survive in New York City. Sure they wanted to see Justice served but I was an innocent man. Accused of a crime I didn't commit.

"Your honor the prosecution calls Officer Stacy to the stand," Gwen said as she put her notes back on the table.

"Officer Stacy, you and you're partner were the first to go upstairs and see Mr. Davis in handcuffs am I right?"

"Yes, we were. He said the female dog China killed an innocent girl and he kept screaming at us about him being robed."

"Mr. Stacy is that how you describe women as female dogs? Because if it is you would be talking about your Mother, Grandmother and even you're ancestors that were Slaves."

"Objection you honor. This has nothing to do with the trail."

"Stained."

Katrina turned around looking at the people in the court room and rolling her eyes at Gwen.

"Officer Stacy, did you or your partner think the defendant was innocent when you arrived at his apartment?"

"Objection your honor she's trying to get him to say something he has no control over."

"Your honor I just what too her Officer Stacy's opinion."

"Your honor he's not qualified to answer that." Gwen said standing up from her table.

"Your honor!" Katrina said.

"Order in the court! Order in the court! First of all the objection is overruled because I want to hear Officer Stacy's opinion."

"Well, when I saw Mr. Davis with both his hands handcuffed and the victim Kim Williams dead right in front of his bed. I had to think reality there was no way Mr. Davis could have committed the crime."

"Thank you, no further questions, your honor." Katrina said as she walked back to the table looking very confident I had to admit Katrina was handling this case very well even though it was her first.

"Ms. Goods, would you like to call anyone else to the stand?"

"Not at this time because they haven't yet arrived here yet."

"Ms. Goods, would you like to call anyone else to the stand?"

"Not at this time your honor."

"Then I suggest we all take a 15-minute break." We will continue in 15 minutes. The Judge said that after seeing how she handled business in the courtroom it gave me a little confidence about her proving my innocence.

After I came out of the restroom I saw Gwen talking on her cell phone. 'Damn that Bitch she knows how much I love working with children how dare she try and ruin my reputation especially when there are so many that look up to me.

"Come Chris clam down I can tell you're nervous but remember it's the Judge who makes the decision, not her."

"Katrina you just don't understand I used to date, Gwen."

"You What? Chris, what were you thinking? I guess I shouldn't be so surprised the way I hear you get around."

I was speechless for a second bit I quickly explained to Katrina that we went out back when Trisha and I were going through our problems. "She was just something on the side."

Katrina pulled me over telling me to keep cool because it had nothing to do with my case.

"Look, Chris, I'm headed to the lady's room just be easy I'm going get you through this."

Before I could take a deep breath Gwen walked up to me. You might've slept with me those few times and stopped calling but even think you're going to have any luck. Because my next witness will prove that you're a very dangerous man." Gwen said as she turned and rolled her eyes at Katrina.

'Lord please don't let it be a cat fight here in court?' Gwen must have been tight at me I wanted to ask her is this case is personal now. I started becoming angry because this case was starting to become one big lust.

"Don't worry Chris Hasson is on his way I need his support and you do also.

"Kalaya will be here also now let's enter this courtroom and prove you're

innocence. "

"Your honor ladies and Gentlemen again we are here to prove that Mr. Chris Davis killed Ms. Kim Williams and sure some may say it was a tragic accident and he had nothing to do with the murder. But as I stated earlier today in this court room justice must be served."

I could tell by the look on their faces that most of those jurors were happy to get a break from work. Then you had some jurors that were there because they had no choice. I'm sure most of them didn't mind being here as long as it was on their time. But in New York City they weren't trying to here that especially if you escaped jury duty the first time. So here we were in court for the second time in one day. I knew some of the jurors in here were saying to themselves how could I've gone through with it? How could I have let two women who were strangers handcuff me, but as I told the Officers it was part of the threesome.

"Your honor my next witness is a woman who knows Mr. Williams very well and in fact, she lives right next door to him."

'Oh my fucking God! Not her? This is one woman I just can't stand. Andrea was a woman I messed around with back when Trisha and I went through our bullshit. She was a lousy fuck, couldn't kiss, and couldn't hold a conversation to save her life. But I didn't have any regrets or apologies.'

The prosecution calls Ms. Andrea Dutch to the stand." Gwen said as she shuffled her papers on her table. Gwen stood at the table while Ms. Dutch was sworn in.

'This isn't good.' I just watched this… This piece of crap went on the stand.

"Ms. Dutch, how do you know the defendant?"

"I'm his next-door neighbor."

"Yes, we already know that, but what the court would like to know is whether Mr. Davis a dangerous to society or not?"

"I wouldn't say he's a threat to society but he is a dangerous man to most women."

"He threatened me the first night I slept with him."

"Why?"

"Because I said I was ready to have a child with him. He also pulled a blade out and put it to my throat saying Bitch I'm not one of those Niggers you can trap."

"Ms. Dutch I will not have that kind of language in my court room. They need to make that N-word and that B-word against the law."

"I'm sorry you're honor but I'm only repeating his exact words."

"No further questions your honor." Gwen said as she walked back to her table.

"You may cross-examine Ms. Hill." The judge said.

Ms. Dutch, how many times have you slept with my client?"

"A few times maybe about 4 or 5 times."

"If my defendant threatened you when you first slept with him why didn't you call the cops and press charges or have an order of protection?"

"I didn't think it was that serious besides the sex was good and I think it was the liquor that made him act the way he did."

"So you're telling me my Client has a drinking problem?"

"No."

"Ms. Dutch, what exactly did you hear in my Clients apartment on the night Kim Williams was killed?"

"Well, I had just gotten out of the shower and I heard a lot of screaming coming from his apartment."

"That's still not telling the Judge or the court what they want to hear. What exactly did hear? Was it a male voice or a female voice you heard?"

"It sounded like a female voice I kept hearing. Please stop! Please stop. I also heard another female voice it almost sounded as if they were arguing."

"Ms. Dutch have you ever experienced a Manjutawa?"

"No, because I'm used to dealing with one man at a time. I'd never go down on another woman."

"Ms. Dutch, would you like to experience a threesome one day?"

"Yes! You only live once."

"Objection you're honor! You're honor what is the point to all of this?" Gwen said letting her objection be known."

"You're honor most people in here have probably never heard of or had a manaja twa, especially with strangers. This is so the Jury can have a better understanding of what my Client has been through."

"Continue Ms. Dutch." The Judge said.

As I said earlier you're honored you only live once. I mean which woman in this world wouldn't want a man's penis in her mouth and vagina at the same time or even in her ass. Ms. Dutch said to the Judge.

"You're honor this... This person's sexual desires have nothing to do with the case we're dealing with." Gwen shouted out.

The Judge cracked a smile before he told Katrina to continue. As I kept looking at the Judge I could tell he wasn't even concentrating on the case anymore.

Ms. Dutch, what is it you do for a living?"

"Well right now I'm unemployed and I'm collecting my unemployment check. But before that, I was working for NYC Transit before I got laid off."

"One more question Ms. Dutch what is it you do in your spare time since you're not working now?"

"Well besides looking for a new job I do the same thing almost every day and night now. I get high while dreaming of a guy like Chris being my Hood Lover. I mean he's nice, friendly, and a role model for children in our neighborhood."

We all waited for the Judge to come back into the courtroom and make a decision if I was guilty or not.

"I haven't decided on this case as of yet, however, we will continue this case in court Friday at 9:00 am see you in two days people." The Judge said as he banged his gavel and the court was dismissed.

The next day while I was coming in for work I noticed how all the kids and their parents were looking at me. I knew they saw the news but this was ridiculous.

As I went into my office to set down I saw Hasan in there waiting for me.

"Damn, every newspaper Hasan this is too much. Whoever wrote this paper has made this article readable damn Hasan."

"Chris don't let it get to you."

I let it be known that it wasn't the article that was getting to me. It was the fact that these parents were putting negative things in these kids' ears about me.

Hasan looked at me with my head down he knew how much I wanted to see these kids get an education. Even though some of them were young parents I still enjoyed giving them the confidence they needed to be successful in life.

As the day went on I realized it was my will to survive and have my innocence proven that kept me working. Also because I had my friend's support

As Hasson and I got off two young teenagers came up tom me Rashawn and Michael. "You're not the role model you claim to be Chris at least that's how a lot of the kids in the neighborhood think. How was your trail?" Michael asked.

Chris, I'm sure you enjoyed your threesome, but why'd you tell us to take it one woman at a time? When you're the one fucking two women at once don't you feel ashamed of yourself?" Rashawn said.

Look what I do behind closed doors is my business and also what I preach to you kids is for your benefit. I said as Hasan and I walked off and headed to my apartment.

"You're not a real role model Chris you've fallen off you're game bro." Michael shouted out.

That hurt coming from those two but they were right in a way. I mean people were blowing this thing out of proportion you would think I was Spider-Man the way the news was making my case.

As Hasson and I got off the elevator in my building my mouth immediately dropped open in surprise. Trisha was right in front of my door with her arms folded. I never knew how much I missed her. Trisha always had that sexy look in her especially when she was ready for some love making.

Wham!

Trisha slapped me in the face and then tried to punch be but I quickly grabbed her arm telling her to calm down. I told Hasan not to worry because I could handle her. Besides I wanted to find out what this was about I quickly opened my door shoving her in my apartment.

What the fuck is you're problem? How dare you embarrass me in front of my boy." I shouted out making sure my words put fear in her heart.

But I was unsuccessful because Trisha jumped in my face screaming…

"How dare you, Chris! After all the investing I put in this relationship! Cooking and cleaning after your sorry-ass half the damn time. How dare you play me like that!"

"What the fuck are you talking about?"

"Don't play dumb with me Chris I saw it on the news and don't you dare tell me it was a bunch off bullshit."

"Look, babe, if you were here instead of Florida none of this shit would've happened. Even if you would've told me you were going none of this would've happened and I wouldn't be going through this bullshit. Now I suggest you get the fuck out of my face and clam down because the next time you swing on me I'm going to forget that you're a woman."

"You're just like all these other men out here Chris you're a fucking dog. Nigger's like you need to be in the dog house, you Rock Weller."

"Well if I'm a dog you must be a dog catcher because I got your ass."

"What?"

"Yeah, this is real talk! If you were satisfying me I wouldn't have had a lustful appetite, especially with your girlfriend Amy, but you're Cousin Josie had the ill pussy. So bitch this is real talk you've proven to be worthless to me. Remember the time I told you the world doesn't revolve around you I meant it."

I quickly escorted Trisha out of my apartment. However, I was still man enough to put her on the train. "So where do we go from here?"

'What the nerve of this Hookier asking me something like that but I guess I had to be a man about it.'

"You're going your way and I'm going mine."

After leaving the train station I went inside the liquor store all of this shit I've been going through is driving me crazy. I called my boy Daniel on his cell phone. Daniel and I haven't spoken in a while since I moved out here to Queens Bridge.

"Hello!" Daniel said.

"Hey, Daniel it's Chris how's it going? I'm surprised you're home."

"Sorry Chris, but you caught me at a bad time. I'm very busy brother starting a company from scratch isn't easy. But I've seen what you've been through on the news. I can only imagine what you've been going through these past few weeks. But Chris I do believe you're innocent."

"Thanks, Daniel but it just got even. That bitch Trisha and I just broke up. She found out about the threesome I had. I even revealed the time I fucked her girlfriend and her cousin but Daniel you know it wouldn't have happened if she wasn't playing those games with me. I swear I almost forgot she was a woman."

I can see that because it's not like you to call her that B word.

Look, Chris, you guys weren't married so just thank her for the education on trusting women such as her because in this era we're in it's the women who are the players. One more thing maybe it was a good thing you broke up because if you had hit her in any kind of way that might have hurt your case. I mean the would've told people you killed Kim Williams."

"Look for the last damn time I didn't kill her. I'm innocent damn it!"

"Look, Chris, I believe you're innocent but you've got to remember it's a game out here. I suggest you buy this book called the games woman play or Cheaters by Eric Jerome Dickey."

I quickly hung up I didn't feel like hearing his preaching I had already brought my liquor. A 5 quarter of E & J and Hennessey.

When I had finally got comfortable in my crib I drank my E&J and rolled up my blunt. 'Damn, this chocolate is some good shit. I've been going through a lot of emotional stress these past few weeks, and today got even worse. Because I lost my Love Trisha and we've broken up for good this time.' As the tears started coming down my eyes I started thinking of some of the things I said to her.

I had proven that I wasn't afraid to say what was on my mind about escaping our relationship. I was down to my last pull on this blunt when Hasan knocked on my door.

The moment I opened the door I heard it immediately. "I don't believe this shit the best man at my wedding in here getting high. And what's with the watery eyes bro?"

What the fuck do you think Hasan? Look at all the shit I'm going through I just broke up with Trisha! I mean how the fuck am I supposed to feel man especially when it was a woman I cared about."

"If you just broke up with Trisha then why are her personal belongings still here?"

"What the hell are you talking about"

"Her G- Strings are still hung up in your room with her name on it."

"Hasan, what are you snoozing around my room for?"

I wasn't! I just went to use it and saw it hanging up.

Look bro don't let this situation brake you down, That's what people are expecting. Especially with your situation, I mean…"

"Hasan just shut the fuck up."

"Look man don't get mad at me. This is you're fucked up shit." Hasan shouted out.

"Hear Nigger have a drink. With the shit, these bitch's put us through you sure could use it."

"Chris that's the Liquor talking, not you. For goodness sack Chris you've got kids that look up to you. Give me the bottle Chris." Hasan said as he attempted to take my E&J bottle.

I quickly snatched it away telling him to leave because he didn't understand what I was going through. Damn, this was my chance to relieve the emotional stress I've been going through. He went out the door without saying a word. I didn't care how upset he was and as I locked my door and turned out all the lights more tears were coming out of my eyes. So I guess it's true what they say men really do cry in the dark.

18

Stacy

I had just got off the phone when Stephan walked into my apartment. Instead of telling me how her first case was going Katrina was preaching to me. She just didn't understand that it was not going to be easy telling him about my job. All I was doing was trying to survive out here in New York City. "Hi, baby what are you doing tonight and why are so dressed up." I asked sitting on my couch.

"I'm doing a show tonight and it's going to be popping in the club tonight."

"At night? Since when?"

I explained to him that I had just got a call to go to work. I quickly reminded him we were going to need the money for our wedding. I was shocked that he didn't argue with me. Instead, he just put his tongue in my mouth and as I collapsed on my couch he let me know the show he was doing tonight was dedicated to me.

I was on the verge of what most of these sisters would call a great life. I had a good man who was about to start his career in the music business. We were planning a wedding and a lot of other things like starting a family buying a house and all that other good shit.

So why the hell was I at a bachelor party shaking my ass in front of all these horny ass Niggers? It's simple people I needed the money, I needed to feel secure.

There was no way I was going to depend on Stephan to make me feel secure. Sure he could help me and all but I wouldn't be happy unless I was making my own money and paying my bills I'm a woman who loves to be independent.

When the song was over I quickly gave the DJ a sign letting him no to play the song I wanted us to perform. The other two females dancing on stage with me took my lead as we were dancing to R-Kelly's song Snake. Karolin was a short slim brown skin woman who was on my left side. She had on a black G-string and a black bra.

Kari was a tall pretty light skin lady she was on my right she also had on a G-string but in the front, it said lick me all over.

We all went out at J-Kemis's Bachelor party. Word was he had a Label coming out and he was one in a million rappers who spoke knowledge. Our boss Baby Cream made plans for us to be here. He made it clear for us to make sure this was the wildest shit these Niggers in here ever seen. When the Reggae music came on we started doing all kinds of moves around J Kemis there was it all out in the open their tongues were licking each one of his earlobes.

Come on J let's head to the VIP room. I said.

"Oh, no sorry ladies, but I love my wife. Go mess with my boys Daniel, Tim, or Komer."

'Damn this Nigga's married? But I guess that's a good thing she's one lucky lady to have one of the faithful men in this world.'

J Kemis pointed us over to where his friends Daniel, Tim, and Komer were. Instead, I suggested that he perform and show us, women, his style.

Baby cream had five more women come inside. We all started dancing while

Kemis was on stage raping too shake your asses.

"Damn, this brother is better than I thought." I said.

We were all doing exactly what Kemis was asking. Karlin and I demonstrated how we women tighten up our butt checks.

After Kemis rapped to three more of his songs each one of us got on stage doing our thing shacking our asses. Some were playing with themselves while Karlin and I were doing our ass-shacking fuck moves.

"That's right Stacy show us how deep your tongue can go inside her." Someone in the room shouted out."

"It can go in big time if I wanted it to." I whispered to Karlin.

"I agree." Karlin said.

Oh shit!" I had just realized who that was who screamed out my name. I spotted him immediately it was Big Mick I went straight to the back telling Brain this show was over.

This show isn't over! Not until I say so do you understand? Brain said as he pulled my arm.

I explained to Brain A.K.A Baby Cream that the tall dark-skinned man smoking that blunt was my man's best friend and I was not about to let this party ruin my relationship. After letting my arm go I pushed Brain in his chest telling him to go fuck himself.

"Bitch who the fuck are you talking to like that? I'll smack the shit out of you. But hitting women isn't in my nature. You just better have my money when you come to work tomorrow."

Brain grabbed my wrist immediately. Look Stacy let's go somewhere and talk after I these ho's home. I know you what some dick tonight."

"Look Brain I've heard and done enough tonight. I'm going home, and by the way, I'm going home and get some great dick from my man."

As I headed out of the club I ran into Big Mike. He was smoking an even bigger blunt than the one before.

I was hoping those three chicks Big Mike was smoking with would keep him busy, but I was wrong because he came and taped me on my shoulder saying… "Stacy

I'm not knocking your hustle but I do expect you to let my boy no what's going. Because if you don't I promise you I will." Big mike said.

"All right Mike, but you've got to promise me you won't tell him you seen me working here."

"It's a deal."

When I arrived home it was 4:00 am in the mourning. I collapsed right on my couch and went to sleep. I was just too tired to be fucking tonight.

The next day as I woke up I reached for my phone to call Stephan, but I didn't get threw he wasn't answering his house or cell phone. 'God I hope Big Mike kept his word on not telling Stephan.'

As I heard in my bathroom to shower my phone started ringing. "Hello?"

"What the fuck you call me for? And where the fuck were you last night you didn't say you were working that long?"

I'm sure anyone of you reading this would no Stephan wasn't in a good mode I had to think fast. And what came to my mind for a situation like this is what most women use as a weapon.

"Okay baby I'm sorry I didn't spend time with you last night but right now I'm horny and my pussy wants that great dick of yours so come get some baby.

When Stephan entered my apartment I could tell by the look on his face that he was still aggravated.

"Come on baby please don't start another argument." I said quickly putting my hand between his legs.

"I'm not angry. I don't get angry there's no need to. Now I will tell you this if you can't discuss things in an adult manner with me than there won't be shit for us to discuss remember that in the future."

I responded by kissing his lips and feeling his manhood. His penis got hard quickly and for the first time, we made love without any rubbers on. Minutes later Stephan kept sucking my nipples I was about to cum and so was he Stephan new it that's why he too his dick out of me. He quickly put three fingers in and out of my wet pussy making me moan again and again.

"Here taste yourself."

I licked my juices reminding him how good I tasted. "Owwwww!"

"Mother fucker that shit hurts," I shouted out.

Stephan went on and quickly spread my legs as far as they could ramming his dick in me. Again he was going in and out but this time his hips were moving along with the process. Ohh." We exploded at the same time damn that shit felt so good. Stephan wasn't thrown yet he turned me over on my stomach grabbed my waist and started hitting my juicy pussy from the back as I laid there on my stomach with his dick grinding in my pussy screaming out his name and telling him to make me cum again.

Within seconds I had multiple orgasms for the first time in my adult life as

we both feel asleep in the missionary position.

Stephan woke me up when his dick had hardened and we were at it again. This time our breathing was heavier than before. "Ohh I love you, baby." As sworn as my pussy had become the love we were making was still in tensed what a wonderful feeling.

We took a shower together washing each other body only a few words were exchanged before we got out. One thing we agreed on was that we both wanted to be married one day. Baby, we should get married at city hall because we'd be saving a lot of money. "You no babe I can't wait to make you my wife. We're going to have a wonderful life together." Stephan said.

That's all I needed to here, because with those words being said I stuck my tongue in his mouth as we stood in the shower kissing each other like we were teenagers and went to bed fucking each other's brains out. It was nice knowing Stephan wanted me to be Mrs. Stephan Powell I guess Katrina and Kalaya were wrong it wasn't important for me to tell Stephan about the work I've been doing at least not now. Because in my two days we'd be Mr. and Mrs. Stephan Powell.

19

Rose

6 weeks later.

"Come on baby you're almost there! Come on you can do it."

"Kenny shut the fuck up I'm the one doing the work here owwww!"

It was time for me to give birth to my baby Kenny drove me to Kings County Hospital.

5 hours later I had just given birth to my son. I quickly named him after my Grand Father Charles Kenny came over and kissed me while I was holding our son in my hands.

"You did a great job baby."

I just smiled at him and told him it was time for us to go home. 30 Minutes later I was told I could go home and as we were driving I was thinking about what had just taken place.

I had just given birth to my first child what a blessing, but before I met Kenny you couldn't have paid me to even think of having a child with these men out here.

Two days had pasted and that's when the arguing started. He kept complaining

The baby looked nothing like him I knew it was time to put this motherfucker in his place reminding him that it was me and him that made our child Charles. I was almost done making dinner when the doorbell rang both Kenny and I looked at each other to see which one of us was going to answer the door.

"Fine, I'll answer it. Look Rose you know I love you and Charles and I'll I'm saying he looks nothing like me. So I suggest we just do the right thing and get a DNA test to see if he's my son."

Not a problem Kenny because I know who I was fucking to have my son. Also, Kenny, when the DNA test is positive, don't be surprised if I kick you out of my house.

"Baby that's just angry talk on your part."

"No Nigger this is real talk so you'd better hope I'm in a good mode when we get these results."

Ding dong, Ding dong.

"Answer the damn door!"

I said as I went to give Charles his milk bottle. I had an idea who was at the door but I wasn't in the mode to see anyone until Kenny and I solved this problem.

It was Katrina Hasson Kalaya and Chris. Kalaya had three bottles of balloons saying it was a boy. Katrina and Hasson had a balloon saying congratulations.

"Hey, what was that yelling we heard? Is everything alright." Katrina asked.

"I'm sorry you'll hear us yelling but Kenny and I were talking about Chris's case." 'I hate to lie but there's one thing I don't tolerate and that's my friends in my business.'

As everyone walked into the living room I handed my son over to his father. But after hearing what Kenny said a few moments ago I was not about to call my Fiancée any time soon.

"So Katrina how's the case going? Did you finally prove Hasson's boy innocent?"

"Not yet the Judge still hasn't made a decision. He said he was going to let both Lawyers no when the case will begin again." Katrina said.

"Well, the important thing is that we all be there to support my boy. It's bad enough some of these kid's parents don't trust him on tutoring or even helping their children anyone."

"Look, Hasson, they don't need to know all of that. I just hope the police catch this bitch. Excuse my language Rose it's just that going back and forth to court can be stressful. Now where here to celebrate you having a healthy new born baby." Chris said.

I could only imagine the stress Chris was going through. Katrina, also I mean from what she told me about their engagement and planning a wedding because of Chris's case.

I didn't feel like eating in the house anymore so I suggested that we go on out and eat dinner. After kissing Kenny and Charles goodbye we all went out to have dinner.

"But we didn't even take pictures of the baby."

"Kalaya there will be other times now let's go."

After we left all I could do was pray that Kenny would be claimed when I came back.

20

Kenny

For the first time in my adult life, I felt like something was wrong in my life. I didn't know how to deal with the situation I guess you could say it was my conscious. I felt bad telling Rose looks nothing like me, but I had, to be honest about it. Isn't that what relationships are about people honest? And I was the kind of man who stuck to his guns so I wasn't about to let Rose no how I felt.

Minutes later my curiosity grew stronger. I sucked my teeth thinking this shit is frustrating. I just couldn't believe Rose would screw a man and get pregnant by him and have me think I was the father. Now don't get me wrong people I love Charles and Rose, but I just have a feeling that Charles isn't my son.

One hour later after feeding Charles, I called the one person that I knew would be honest with me. Seconds later I was getting the third degree and listening to a whole lot of preaching.

"But ma I'm telling you Charles looks nothing like me. I just can't believe Rose would put me through this shit. She knew how badly I wanted a family. That just goes to show people do take kindness for weakness and…"

My Mother interrupted me. "Kenny things happen. Now if Rose knew she was pregnant before you two started making Charles then shame on her. But I doubt seriously that she would even go there. Now, Kenny, you and your brother are strong and special and have a lot to offer your families you and Rose work through your problems."

"Don't worry ma we will." I said.

"And how do you plan on doing that."

"I already told her we're getting a blood test done, and we'll see if he is my child. I mean it's crazy ma these women or today are crazy that's why Kayne west came out with the song Gold digger."

"Hush boy! Don't ever let me hear you talk like that ever again."

"No ma, I am going to talk how I feel, because I'm not going to go through with what these men on these TV shows go through. I mean it's one thing to choose the man you want to have a child with, but to have that man thinking he's the father of a child when he's not. Do you know the emotional pain and stress that causes?"

"Son like I said things happen."

"Look Mother Charles is crying I think he needs a diaper change I'll talk with you later."

After reminding my Mother how much I loved her. I went to change Charles's diaper and put him to sleep as I looked around our room I thought about the good times Rose and I had together. Before Charles was born we were always going to dinner dancing at clubs together we did it all together.

While I was lying in bed ready to fall asleep I started thinking of all the women I was involved with before I met Rose. The majority of them were about money, money, money, or how much you were willing to spend on them. It also depended on the kind of car I drove.

For example, my ex-girlfriend Tracy was a sexy attractive brown-skinned woman who weighed about 150. Her thing was spend, spend, spend and most men including

myself had to pay to play. I would always have to spend money on her just to get some. She'd pay for dinner once in a while but the majority of our relationship was about her spending money I finally told her how I felt and broke up with her.

'Damn some brothers are never satisfied and when they are women just do or say something tom make that man put his guard back up.' I said before falling asleep.

When I woke up and looked at the time it was a little after 2 in the mourning. Rose still hadn't come home. 'Damn, she's lucky I don't have to work tonight.'

After turning all the lights out I lied down holding Charles in my arms thinking should I seek counseling or just leave Rose and Charles altogether I'm sure you'll reading this knew I'd choose option number 1 because I love Rose too much to just walk out. And even though Charles looks nothing like me I'm still going to be her to see if he's mine or not, but as my mother said home is where your heart is I mean a man's home is like his castle and that's why he should be treated like a king.

As I was about to close my eyes Rose came in the house. "Baby I'm home."

She said as she kissed me.

"How is everything luv" I asked.

"Everything's fine baby but I have to tell you I'm tired of all this arguing we've been doing. So after I put Charles in his baby carriage it's time for some serious love making."

"I hear you, babe." I said as I pulled Mr. Valentine out letting her know I was ready.

Within seconds Rose was screaming. "Oh… God, Oh my fucking God Mother fucker what happened to my baby?"

I put my boxes back on and went straight to Charles's room. "Babe what's wrong?"

Mother fucker my baby has a fever feel his damn head and you're asking me what's wrong.

"Now Kenny I know you don't think Charles is your child but you could've told me he had a fever."

"Look just clam down."

"You expect me to calm down when my baby has a fever. All I asked you to do was watch your son for a while Damn it I swear men don't know a damn thing when it comes to taking care of a baby and making sure they're healthy."

'Fuck now that hurt. I've never heard Rose talk to me like this. I got so pissed off I punched the wall and ended up putting a hole in it.

I don't know what made me think I was getting some pussy tonight. I guess what some parents say is true once the baby is born it is not about the Mother and Father anymore.

As we rushed out the door into a cab headed to Kings County Hospital I prayed that Charles would be alright and I wanted a DNA test to be positive because then I would no longer second guess myself or our relationship.

Although Rose's not like the women of today I still had to be sure about Charles and make sure he's my child. 'Lord help me please?'

I continued to hold Rose in my arms kissing her on her lips letting her no everything will be alright because I love Charles no matter what For the first time I did something I thought I'd never do which was cry in front of a woman.

21

Rose

20 minutes later we were in Kings County Hospital waiting for the doctor to tell me what was wrong with my baby. Kenny couldn't stand my mouth so I knew the cab driver couldn't but he still kept his focus. I was cursing so much in the cab that Kenny kept trying to kiss me just to shut my mouth up. Although he had tears in his eyes which I thought was beautiful I was just too worried about Charles. That's just how we Mothers are especially with our first child. Drive motherfucker, drive this mother fucking cab my baby needs a doctor. The cab had to be going at least 55-60 and it was a good thing there wasn't too much traffic I believe God was with us on this one.

Moments later as we kept waiting for the doctor to come tell us something Kenny kept trying to comfort me, but I was too upset to even speak to Kenny all I kept thinking about was my baby. 'Might as well get this blood test over with also.'

Two days later I was at home with my son in tears I felt like such a fool. How could this have happened I kept repeating to myself. Right before we left the Hospital the other night Kenny and Charles had a DNA test done. We got the results yesterday and I've been in been in tears ever since. Kenny was frustrated and I couldn't blame him. Finding out Charles wasn't his put a knife to his heart but I always reminded him this was a misunderstanding. I felt so ashamed of myself Kenny hasn't spoken to me at all every time he comes home he goes straight to sleep from those doubles he's been doing. Charles was sound asleep so that gave me a little time to be alone and think although I still felt miserable and lousy.

The phone rang and I had a feeling who it was. It was Katrina and Kalaya they were calling me all day to see if me and my son were alright because of what I told them. They both wanted to come over here but I didn't want any company. I didn't feel like being around anyone.

I just didn't understand. I've been faithful in this whole relationship with Kenny. "Shit! I finally found my Mr. Right there was no reason for me to be unfaithful to Kenny. And Every Nigger I fucked I made sure they used protection. Ohh shit!" Someone had just come to mind.

Moments later as I was headed out my apartment with my son Kenny was at the door.

"Look Rose I realize Charles isn't my son but I'd be happy to adopt him and call him my son. Because sweetie if we were going to raise Charles I want us to have love and communication in our home."

I looked at Kenny telling him the same thing and reminding him that it takes two.

"I'm letting you know now Kenny it takes a strong brother to do want you're doing. That's why I'm glad you're mine."

"Rose you don't even have to tell me something I already no. You don't have to question my manhood because I've never been so sure of anything in my life trust me, babe, everything will be fine."

I gave him half of a smile telling him I had an idea who the father of Charles is.

"Then let's go see him together."

9o Minutes later both Kenny Charles and I were in front of his door knocking he came out of the elevator with whom I believed to be his fiancé.

"Hi, Travis it's been a long time."

"Rose, how have you been? Wow! Is this the little man you two brought into the world? Congratulations."

"Yes it is but we needed to talk and it would be best that you're fiancé here what Kenny and I have to say."

"Can't this wait I mean this is bad timing on your part."

"Travis, what's going on? Have you been fucking around all of a sudden?" His fiancé Monica asked.

"No honey it's nothing like that."

Moments later we were in Travis's living room and after introducing myself and Kenny to Monica I got right to the point. Kenny placed his arm around me while I held Charles in my arm. And it was a good thing Monica was home because I wanted her to here this for herself.

"Travis remember where I was pregnant I thought I was carrying Kenny's baby, but it turned out to be someone else, and that someone is you."

"What?" Travis shouted out.

"What?" Monica said.

"What do you mean my child? You and I have never had sexual intercourse except… Oh shit!"

"Rose, who else were you messing with?" Travis asked with a smile.

"Don't play yourself, Motherfucker, it's your baby. And if you don't, believe me, you can have a DNA test done just like Kenny did, but I will let you no Kenny will be in our son's life."

All of a sudden Travis's arms unfolded both he and Monica had a surprised look on their faces emotions came across Travis's face.

"Oh my God Travis! This is a surprise but I believe you because you wouldn't have gone through all this trouble."

I watched Travis kiss Monica and jump up in the air. Shouting… "I'm a Father! Yeah, I'm a Father."

Monica's expression was mixed with anger and hurt I wanted to say something but I felt I had to say something but I felt I had said enough. Monica started to cry Damn! The things we women have to live and deal with it just aren't right but I had to deal with it and let my man no. Monica had to make the same choice which was to stay or let him go.

22

Hassan

"Noooo!"

Hassan baby are you alright? That's the second time this week.

Katrina was right it was the second nightmare and that's twice this week I've jumped out of bed screaming about it. That wanna-be gangster bitch in China has been on my mind lately. Ever since my boy Chris's case, it's been making me think back to when my brother was murdered.

"Hassan are you all right?" Katrina asked.

"Hassan."

"Hassan." Katrina shouted out.

"I'm … I'm sorry baby it's just that… that I've been doing a lot of thinking lately."

"You're not having second thoughts about us are you?" Katrina asked with a concerned look.

"No…No baby. I swear to God! I've never been so sure about anything in my life. I can't wait to make you Mrs. Hassan Johnson, but right now I need you to bear with me." I said as we both sat up on our bed.

30 Minutes later both Katrina and I were rolling over and kissing each other and I enjoyed every minute of it. I loved a woman who listened to what I had to say. That's what made Katrina special to me.

It didn't surprise me at all but I knew I'd tell Katrina sooner or later about my bothers death. But that's one of the reasons I proposed to Katrina because we've been able to communicate with each other I can talk to her about anything. So bringing up my bothers death wasn't a problem. The problem was that Chris's case somehow reminded me of my brother's death and that's the reason it's been hard to sleep this week.

Soon I started kissing my way down to her breast as she moaned with pleasure and excitement. I went down to her stomach and then to her womanhood, but to no surprise, she grabbed my head and started calling out my name.

"Oh...Oh... Hassan."

Her breathing became heavier I had my tongue doing tricks in her walls that other women could only imagine their man doing to them. Katrina kept easing

her legs which made it much easier for me, but this time she was squeezing my head.

"Baby Chill and relax pleasure." I said.

"Hassan you'd better finish want you started because I'm not going to stop when it's my turn."

What the hell! After she listened to me and because she's been dealing with Chris's case Katrina was entitled to receive this pleasure.

A few moments later Katrina had finally exploded. After Katrina had gained her composure she started placing kisses on my chest and then found her way to my manhood.

Damn, this shit feels so good!

"Ohh...Damn baby oh... yeah." I was holding onto the sheets with everything I had in me. My woman had skills in the bedroom and knew how to give pleasure as well as receive it.

Soon we were in the 69 position pleasing each other as if we were going for a gold medal. My hands were all over her ass while I was getting my freak on. As for Katrina, it felt as though she was trying to swallow my dick.

"Oh…Hassan, I'm about to cum again!" Katrina said.

"I'm about too cum too baby!" I said as I tired catching my breath.

We both exploded and watched it trick down our thighs. As freaky as Katrina was in the bedroom I wanted her to remember I was freakier. I licked her thighs and went right back to the entrée.

"No more Hassan! No more at least no more with your tongue."

I knew what that meant, but I looked at the time and saw it was 5:00 a.m. I let Katrina no what time it was and that we'd have to get ready for work soon but she insisted that we finish getting buck wild. I was placing kisses on her back as I kept fucking her. Katrina couldn't tell what was coming next because I kept switching

up on her. From fast to slow and as I switched from fast again I felt myself getting even deeper as the moans were getting louder.

Minutes later Katrina screamed out she was ready to explode again.

Me too! I said. And we did just that except this time it was much more pleasurable. I guess it was because we didn't have protection on but it damn sure felt great. We stayed in each other's arms and felt asleep until the alarm went off at 7: ooam.

'Damn time for work.'

I quickly gave Katrina a mourning kiss. How about some breakfast in bed babe?

"How thoughtful of you baby but not today Hassan I've got a lot of paper work to do at the office today, but you can cook for us while I take my shower."

A few minutes later both Katrina and I were at the table having breakfast.

"You no Hassan at first I was nervous when I took this case but no I'm so close to proving Chris's innocent."

"Once again I congratulated my woman letting her no to keep up the good work because just we knew Chris was going to need a whole lot of luck. I was very happy to see this case wasn't taking its toll on Katrina as I thought it would.

There's one thing we men forget when we have a good lady in our life. We forget the things they go through and the things they do for us. Katrina made me want to be a better man for her I kissed her letting her know that when no one was around for her I'd be there for her.

We both got on the F train and headed to work I frowned and shook my head thinking about the dream I had earlier. I thought I would forget about it but there were images of my brother's murderer in my head. I wanted to talk to her about opening my nonprofit recreation center for kids and young adults. But I could never bring up the subject.

I guess you could say I had issues to deal with.

Although I was one of the men in the world that kept my issues a secret I knew sooner or later I'd have to tell Katrina about what I'd been going through.

Baby you no sooner or later we're going to have to start making wedding plans." "Baby!"

"Hassan! Hassan! Are you alright? Did you hear anything I had to say?"

Katrina quickly had a concerned look on her face but I quickly kissed her telling her not to worry.

"Come on Hassan I know when something's brothering you. Now tell me what it is?"

Suddenly Katrina's voice got louder and we quickly drew a crowd waiting to see what would happen next. But I got lucky because my stop came up.

"What is it, Hassan? Has my father been threatening you again?"

I kissed her again this time on her cheek and reminding her we both had to go to work so it was best we discuss this later.

"Sister you going to let him leave without giving you an explanation. I wouldn't

Put up with that if I were you." A woman shouted out.

'Damn if I wasn't such a gentleman I'd curse that nosey ass woman out and hurt her feelings.' I said to myself as I got off the train.

When I got in my office Chris was right there waiting for me with a huge smile on his face. I shook my head although Chris was like a brother to and I loved him to death but nowadays he was just hard to figure out.

"Hassan its official! I'm sure I can win and get my respect back, especially from these kids. God is with me I'm sure I'll get through this."

I just looked at Chris although I was happy for him I just wasn't in the mood.

"Hassan what's the matter bro don't sit here and lie to me."

"Chill out man."

Chris could tell when something was bothering me. I quickly took a deep breath and told him everything.

"Man, that's deep."

Chris quickly put his hand on my shoulder telling me to just be a man about it.

"Man you and Katrina are about to be husband and wife and your marriage is going to work communication is one of the keys to a happy marriage."

Now did you hear that this is coming from a guy I no to be the player of all players? It's funny how we men can talk about our issues with each other but not our women. I mean we'll keep issues inside before we tell someone we're going through

something. I guess did find God. I let him no he was 100% right and that I'd tell Katrina about the problem later.

As the day went on I felt more relaxed and more comfortable. It was after 3:00 pm and now was the time the kids came for school.

It didn't matter if they were in high school, junior high school or Elementary school, because here we made sure they were going in the right direction in life. Ok, Hassan let's do this." I said.

As I got up out of my chair I saw Susan. It was Susan's last year of High school I was very happy when she told me she was accepted to John Jay College. She was looking like she wasn't in the mood for my advice. Instead, she walked up to me telling me how much of a great listener I am.

"Hassan you've always been there when I needed a friend or just someone to talk too. And for that, I want to thank you."

"Not a problem. You know I love helping people out."

Susan quickly told me what was on her mind and as usual wanted advice just to make sure she was doing the right thing.

I let her know that she was making the right decision and that her man should never encourage her to smoke. To make matters worse he was trying to persuade her not to go to college because he wanted them to start a family.

"Susan if this guy loves you like you've been telling me he should have the patience for you. Come on Susan you know you're education comes first and you know what drugs do to your body. That shit can even stop you from getting a good-paying job."

She quickly closed the door and blinds at the door. When she turned back around nothing but her bra was showing.

Hassan did you ever fantasize about having sex and doing other freaky shit with me."

"What?"

I quickly raised both of my eyebrows, because I couldn't believe this was happening although Susan had a banging body I was always aware of her having a curse on me but I never expected it to lead to this.

Susan, you're a beautiful young woman and have a great heart and have the perfect man waiting for you."

"Hassan look at me. Look at this body don't you realize you're the man for me?

"I'm legal now remember my birthday was last month."

"Susan I'm truly honored that you find me attractive and all that other shit and if I was younger maybe I'd go out with you. But…"

Before I could say another word Susan grabbed the back of my neck and out her tongue in my mouth she immediately had her tongue dancing in my mouth.

"Hey, Hassan guest who stop by wow!!"

Before I could push Susan off of me and talk some sense into her Chris came storming into my office escorting the last person I would have ever expected.

It was Katrina's father he ran up to me grabbing me by my shirt.

"Just when I started having respect for your ass dread and you're here about to screw one of your so-called students. If I were her father I'd have your ass arrested."

"Now wait a moment Mr. Johnson I'm sure there's an explanation to all of this." Chris said.

"He's right Mr. Johnson believe me this is all just a misunderstanding."

"A misunderstanding that's not what I saw. I mean look at the way she's looking at you dreaded ass, and you expect to marry my daughter."

As I turned my head Susan had tears in her eyes I told her it was time for her to leave and go home. When Susan was gone I quickly closed the door.

"Now Mr. Johnson 1st of all I do intend to marry your daughter. Second I told you, Chris, before this is all a misunderstanding third it was her who kissed."

"A misunderstanding that's not what I just saw. I mean look at the way she's looking at you dreaded ass and you expect to marry my daughter."

When I turned my head I saw Susan with tears in her eyes. I told her it was time for her to leave and go home.

When Susan was gone I quickly closed the door looking at Katrina's father.

"Now Mr. Johnson 1st of all I do intend to marry your daughter. Second I told you and Chris before this is all a misunderstanding third it was her who kissed me."

Katrina's father just gave me a stare balling up his fist. Now I know this old man didn't think he was going to wipe my ass. "Hassan you've got three choices 1 you either tell my daughter what occurred here or I will. 2 You either call off this engagement or I'm going to tell her because in my book you two shouldn't be getting married if the first place. I mean how do you plan on supporting each other? Are you ready for the reasonability that comes with marriage?"

Before Mr. Johnson could finish I cut him off. "Mr. Johnson you no something I don't even care what you think about me. I don't care if you feel like I'm not right for your daughter. Yes, I live in a place most people call the Hood. Now as I said to you it was Susan who came onto me. Now she came here looking for help and advice. Do you think I'd jeopardize my job and something I love doing?" "What? Were you helping her with sexual healing?"

"Look! What you saw wasn't supposed to happen."

Chris stepped in between the both of us looking both of us in the face telling us we weren't getting anywhere with this arguing.

"Hassan you're the adult you're supposed to be prepared for something like that. You should've known Susan was attracted to you. I mean half the women here are, but you're too blind to notice it."

I raised both eye brows at Chris and looked at Katrina's father as he just gave me a stare. "Look, Hassan, I believe you but remember what I to you. Either you tell my daughter or I will. Also, remember what I said 2 and 3 were."

Once Katrina's father left I shook my head explaining to Chris exactly what happened. "Look, bro, you should need too just be a man about it and confess to Katrina. Tell her everything bro what's been bothering you. What occurred today we'll meet her and Kalaya at the Sin city club and remember what I said just be a man about it."

Chris had talked me into coming to the Sin City club. I had no idea Katrina and Kalaya's friend Stacy worked here. Although Stacy had a banging body and had just about every man's eyes on her watching her do her thing just wasn't what I was focused on. Both Chris and I sat at the bar waiting for Katrina and Kalaya to show up. "Hassan, what's wrong bro? Why are you so quiet? Look, Hassan, I'm here for you bro so try to think positive." I just gave Chris a stare, but before I could say something Katrina came up from behind and planted kisses on my neck. "Hi, babe. How are you?" Katrina asked.

"I'm fine babe, how are you? How was your day? And hello to you too Kalaya I never knew you're friend Stacy worked here."

She's been here for a while. Why do you two enjoy watching her shack her ass? Kalaya asked.

Both Chris and I just gave each other a stare and cracked a smile. Now I know you ladies are expecting us to be honest, but Chris and I both know how jealous women can be towards each other.

They just gave serious looks. "Look why don't you two ladies just chill, besides Katrina I think it's time you and Hassan talk Kalaya may I have this dance?"

'Damn you, Chris.' I didn't know whether Chris was trying to be funny or not, but

Both Chris and Kalaya went to the dance floor and the song that was playing was Usher's Song Confession.

"Hassan, what is Chris talking about?"

I looked at Katrina in the face and all I could think about was what Chris said earlier which was just be a man about it.

I had a look at the shack for a moment. That couldn't be her. It's just not possible. Either the woman I was seeing was a Chameleon or that was China herself.

23
Katrina

I watched Hassan's facial expression change. I was tempted to pull him over to the side so he could tell me what was wrong with him. But Chris came up to me he saw Kim's murderer. "Are you sure Chris?"
Of course Katrina I'd never forget that bitch's face. That's China over there she's the one who killed Kim. Believe me, she better be lucky I'm a man of God or I'd go over there and fuck her ass up right now woman or not."
"Chris just clam down. Kalaya you call the cops Hassan we're still going to have that talk. I see her headed to the lady's room with another woman. I'm going to make sure she doesn't catch another body."
I went into the lady's room with a plan in mind I had just brought a new tape recorder although I was a little nervous, but this was part of being a lawyer, and proving Chris's innocent's was important to me.
"Now if you want to end up like that bitch Kim did I'd suggest you do as I say."
"China you know I won't play you. I just need some Dick you know the real thing and you know I'll do a good job."
"Long as you no that's my pussy and long as you do not too fall in love with any of these Niggas out here. That's why I killed Kim the bitch was falling in love with a Nigga she just met. And I fucked the shit out of that Nigga while she bleed to death. Now go out there and get that Nigga so we can do this."

I heard every word China said and even recorded it. The two of them were laughing and celebrating as if they'd get away with this. They should've known God doesn't like ugly.

It was a good thing I was pretending to be shitting. When I heard them leave the lady's room I called Kalaya on her cell immediately to make sure the cops already arrived. "Yes, that's what I'm talking about. Ohh... Wow."

I ran right back to the toilet and threw up. 'No, not now I'm just hoping this is from something I eat.'

As I came out of the ladies room I heard a lot of yelling. "I'm innocent! You Mother fuckers, can't hold me against my will. I'm fucking innocent please you've got to believe me."

After making my way through the crowd I played the tape I had just recorded.

I also had to let the police know who I was and what I did.

The tape played. 'That's why I killed Kim the bitch was falling in love with the Nigga she just met.'

"Nice work Katrina," Chris said.

Right after the two Police officers read China her rights both Hassan and Chris walked up to China. "I told you Bitch you can't run from Justice."

Hassan grabbed Chris's shoulder telling him too clam down. "You no China you could've prevented all of this from happening. You could've even gotten yourself some help if you would've turned yourself in."

Now I'm looking forward to going to court. Let's see how this bitch loves being on the stands." Chris shouted out.

Tears were coming out of China's eyes she turned around looking at Hassan and the rest of us. "You know I should've got help a very long time ago. But I was never around positive people like you are."

"Come on it's time for you to go to the percent."

"Wait Officer please let's hear what she has to say," Hassan said.

"Who gives a fuck what this bitch has to say?"

"Chris chill out man. China continue, please.

"You'll don't understand, I'm from the Hood. That fucking chain you're boy Chris has on that Nigga would easily get robed for it. So you'll see I had no choice but to hustle."

My GrandMother was too old to raise me because of my fucking mother doing time for killing an ex- boyfriend she murdered."

"I'm curious what was this guy's name who your Mother murdered."

"What's with all these Damn questions all of a sudden? You'll ask my girl?"

"Look bitch your girl's going to have to go to court anyway so she might as well." answer the questions.

I could understand where Chris was coming from. With all this hate towards China and her friend have. But, I had no clue as to why Hassan was asking all these questions. He even went over to wipe her tears away. 'What was that all about?'

Ladies don't think for a second I was letting this shit slide. Hassan was going to hear my mouth before this day was over but right now I had to keep it professional

I couldn't let drama ruin Chris's case.

"Now China tell me what's your Mother's name?" Hassan asked.

"Why should I give that bitch's gov't name out? She was never there to raise me anyway."

"Please China the name?"

"Fine her name was Marry Powell."

That's enough questioning people it's time for her to go to the percent. The officer said before he got in the police car and drove off.

There was no sign of happiness on Hassan's face. I could tell he was stunned, but for what we all watched as the police car drove off.

"Hey you everybody is everything alright Stacy asked.

"You're late Stacy, but we're all right thank you." Kalaya said.

One hour later both Hassan and I were arguing. I became so agitated I just couldn't take it anymore.

"Why do you keep questioning me?"

"Because you're ass won't tell me what's bothering you. Do you have something to hide or are you fucking some other woman? Maybe like China."

I'm tired of you asking all these questions all of a sudden. Hassan shouted out.

He paused taking a deep breath. "Look it's my problem, not yours now please just let it go."

No, I won't I'm here to help and be here for you. Damn it, Hassan, I'm not walking into a marriage with my man feeling guilty about something he should have never done or allowed to happen. What happened to communication I see you reading that Black Love Entertainment magazine all the time haven't you learned anything from it."

I might have gone too far by saying that because Hassan's face quickly changed.

Katrina, there is nothing you can do to help me it's my problem look the only thing you can do for me that will bother me is make me very unhappy and right now you're doing just that."

'How cold all the time I've known Hassan he's never talked to me this way. Much less say anything that would hurt me. A tear came down my face and quickly I was in Hassan's arms crying.

"Ok, ok you win I should've known better than too argue with you."

Hassan quickly came over hugging me as he handed me a piece of tissue.

I quickly shoved him off and threw the tissue to the floor.

"Hassan I'm not your girlfriend I'm you're a woman. We're engaged for God to shake. All I'm asking is for you to tell me what's been bothering you. How do you expect us to grow old with each other if we're not communicating with one another?"

Hassan sat me on his bed holding my hand. "Katrina today's been a very rough day for me. All day you've been asking what's wrong with me and I know you were just being concerned and that's another example of you just showing your love for me and I want you to know I love you." Hassan said as his lips touched mine.

"Hassan don't try too clam me down with a kiss just tell me what's been bothering you. Is it that bad that you weren't going to tell me?"

Hassan kissed me again. This time his tongue went deep in my mouth.

"Wait a moment Katrina who was that woman China said was never there for her?"

"Her Mother."

"Yes! I t appears that her mother is the one who killed my brother all those years ago. So you can see now where China got her female pimping from."

My mouth was wide open there was nothing left for me to ask. I quickly hugged Hassan telling him how sorry I was for making him tell me and what was on his mind.

I had never felt this insecure before it was like I was going through a change. "Katrina that's not all I have to discuss with you." He paused taking a deep breath. I quickly exhaled.

Moments later "How the fuck could you allow that to happen?"

"Katrina if you…"

"You're a fucking adult Hassan. You should've seen it coming and you expect me to believe you did nothing to instigate her actions."

Hassan just looked at me shaking his head as his facial expression quickly changed. "Hold on Katrina I swear to you I did no such thing and it was best that I told you this and not your father."

"What? My Father knew about this? That's just great, that's the last thing I needed was for my family to be in my business."

As we looked each other in the face Hassan started telling me everything that went down at work. He even told my Father to tell me if he didn't. I knew my father was just protecting me but putting that kind of pressure on Hassan was too much.

I kept starring at Hassan and listening to what he had to say. Finally, he started smiling at me.

"Look Katrina I swear to you I'd never do anything to jeopardize what we have. I always promised myself that if I found that special someone all these other women wouldn't mean a thing to me so stop worrying because you're not going to lose me.

Katrina haven't I told you I'm in love with you? So don't let a little kiss destroy us."

I immediately put a finger on his lips. "Hassan I believe you, and I want you to hear what I have to say. To that girl that was more than a kiss. Believe me, I was a teenager myself so I know now if you'll excuse me I'm going to the bathroom."

It was obvious from the way Hassan was explaining himself to me that he never expected Kim to do what she did. And it was obvious that my suspension was right.

It was a good thing I went to Duane reed earlier I was pregnant but how was I going to tell Hassan I already knew he'd say to me to take it easy while I'm in court.

As I came out of the bathroom Hassan was right there at the door waiting for me to come out.

"Are you alright Katrina?"

I ignored him and made my way to the kitchen.

"Katrina!" Hassan shouted out. "Tell me what's bothering you. Is that kiss still bothering you, because if it is I'm telling you for the last time it meant nothing."

As I opened the refrigerator door Hassan turned me around. Here let me show you what a real kiss is."

I quickly turned my head not letting his lips touch mine.

"Katrina, what's the problem?" Hassan shouted out.

I heard you the first time. I said as a tear came down my left eye.

"Then tell me."

"I'm pregnant. Here's the pregnancy test I just took and it shows that I'm

pregnant. Yes, Hassan, I'm carrying your child."

Hassan had a stunned look on his face but what could he say I had the proof right there in his face. Suddenly there was a look of excitement on Hassan's face one I had never seen on him before. His hole hand slapped my ass. "Baby that's wonderful news."

What do you mean? You're not upset?" Pow!

Hassan slapped my ass even harder than before. Of course, I'm not upset I tell

You baby I can't wait to make you my wife and I can't wait to make us a true family.

It was obvious from the way Hassan kept smiling that he wanted this child. He told me this was a gift from God.

90 Minutes later. That's what I loved about the love-making Hassan and I always made especially Hassan he always makes sure I'm satisfied. I always make sure his happy. But Hassan always makes sure I cum and that lady is the love of a great man one who doesn't think about his needs. "I love you, Katrina."

"I love you too Hassan." I said as I buried my tongue in his mouth because the love making we just made was something to remember.

24
Chris

Two weeks had pasted since I last saw Hassan and Katrina. I was real happy for both of them because not only were they engaged but they were expecting a child in another 8 months. As for myself, I was in court tomorrow and it was something I was looking forward too. Finally, my innocence would be proven and finally, those false remarks about me would be put to rest.

Ding. 'Earlier than I expected.' I already knew who it was and as I opened the door Kalaya was right there wearing blue Sean John jeans and a matching jacket. Kalaya and I had been seeing each other for about 3 weeks. I knew I had surprised her when I told her when we have sex I want it to be special. She respected me for that and told me she wouldn't do anything to bring out the evil that was once inside me. We were honest with each other from the jump start. I told her to leave Evil C in the grave yard and everything will be fine.

While she was in the kitchen fixing our plates with the KFC she brought I was on my couch thinking. Kalaya was everything I ever wanted in a woman she showed compassion she was funny loyal smart and tonight I was going to find out how freaky she could be. I was falling for Kalaya more and more every day. Especially how she stuck by me even before we were dating she believed that I was innocent.

Kalaya gently put our plates on the table and gave me one of her passionate tried putting too fingers inside her but she grabbed my waist saying… "Chris don't start something you're not going to finish."

"Oh, I intend to finish trust me," I said smiling.

"After we eat baby it's on." She said giggling.

'Good because I couldn't wait to get into those jeans.'

Moments later Kalaya came out of my bedroom in a sexy red thong to watch Daddy's little girl with me. We sat there codling and enjoying the movie. Kalaya you don't know how much I'm looking forward to being in the court room and."

Before I could say another word Kalaya ran her fingers over my head telling me to relax because anything can happen in court.

Let's not talk about court right now." She said with a smile

"Chris what does a girl have to do get some loving around here."

"Kalaya you're a beautiful woman don't ever forget that." I said as I felt the warmth of her lips. I no Kalaya couldn't resist me but I had to stop myself.

"Chris, what's the matter?" Kalaya asked as she ran her fingers across my head for the second time.

"You know Kalaya it's not even important anymore." I said as we started exploring each other which led to me unbuckling my belt.

I started sucking her hardened nipples while Kalaya was playing with my manhood. I watched Kalaya go to work and before she even put me inside of her, her lips were on my manhood God damn! The shit felt so good I'm glad I went along with what Kalaya suggested. I had wanted us to do the 69, but she didn't what that. She wanted to do me first and she wanted to be very focused when it was my turn to please her.

20 Minutes had passed and I had Kalaya's legs spread wide open. She started moaning from just me putting three of my fingers inside her. I

quickly put one of my other fingers over her mouth to smooth her moans. Kalaya let out one hell of a loud moan once my tongue was inside her. With every taste of Kalaya's vagina came louder and louder moans. I started slowing my licks down, but Kalaya quickly grabbed my head.

"Chris don't stop Owwwww."

"Mmmmmm." I put my hole hand over her mouth.

"Damn girl, you want the whole Queens Bridge to cheer you? Jesus just clam down."

Chris didn't I tell you not to start something you can't finish."

Be easy Kalaya and relax because it's about to get hot and wet in here. I said as I kept palming her ass she looked at me smiling.

"Wait Chris stop don't you hear that?"

"Hear what?"

"Someone is knocking on your door."

I endured her putting her in the dogging-style position. Because you'd better believe I was going to finish what I started.

Kalaya turned around facing me. "Chris I'm serious there's someone at your door. Now answer it because it could be Katrina with news about your case."

"Fine."

Katrina both you and Hassan have the worst timing. I swung the door open and immediately gasped, Because of who it was.

"Trisha?"

I stood there like a fool shaking my head. Trisha, what are you doing here?"

I said eyeing her suspiciously with a suit case she had in her hand. Chris, what's the matter Aren't you glad to see me? She said dropping her suitcase and wrapping her arms around me.

I quickly shove her off me telling her that it wasn't a good time. I noticed there was a bandage around her arm.

"Look, Chris, I just need to talk with you for a few minutes."

"Look Trisha now isn't a good time."

"Well, can't you make it a good time? Come on Chris don't you miss me?"Trisha hadn't changed a bit. She still had that determination in her. Especially when things didn't go her way she'd try her best to make sure they do. She tried pushing her way past me and entering my crib but I cut her off. "Look, Trisha, I've got company now you're going to have to come some other time."

"What? Don't tell me your fucking some hookier in there?"

"And if I am it's none of your business." I said raising my voice.

Before I could say another word Kalaya came to the door in a red T-shirt asking if was everything alright.

Now, will you tell me your reason for coming here?" I asked holding Kalaya in my arms in front of Trisha. Trisha gave us both of her jealous looks.

"Ok! But first, let me say, Chris, I should have never let you out of my life. Will you ever forgive me?"

Kalaya quickly gave her a look folding her arms. It was obvious Kalaya heard what Trisha called her. "Look, Chris, I'm sorry for coming here unannounced but I had to tell you how I feel. Chris I know I did you wrong and running out of your life made things worse but will you ever forgive me?"

I felt like laughing but instead, I told her I'd forgive her. Shit! I had already forgiven her I would not be a man of God if I didn't forgive her but I would never forget the pain she put me through.

"I'll forgive you, Trisha, now tell me the real reason you're doing here and what's with the suitcase?"

"Ok fine. I've broken up with my boyfriend. I've gotten tired of his abusiveness. Chris, do you see this?"

Trisha unwrapped the bandage that was on her arm. Both Kalaya and I saw 13 stitches she had on her arm. Usually, I would have busted out laughing but I was a changed man.

Before Kalaya and I could say another word Officer Green came on the elevator.

"Well! Well! What do we have here?"

Kalaya stormed to the bedroom to put on some clothes. "What can I do for you Officer Green?"

Well, Mr. Williams, I came here to apologize for not believing your innocents but it appears I might have been right about you handcuffing yourself just to cover your ass." Officer Green said while looking at Trisha's stitches.

"Lord help me now!" I shouted out.

Officer Green, what makes you think I did something to this woman?" I paused looking him in the face.

"Look Officer Green you only think I'm a suspect probably because it's Thursday. It's the day most of you Cops look to arrest people."

"No I'm not and for the record arresting people is part of the job. Now I'm here to find out what happened to this woman's arm."

"Then ask her." Kalaya said giving Officer Green a stare and Trisha a more evil one.

After telling Officer Green what happened. He suggested Trisha come fill out a police report. She quickly refused but I quickly convinced her it was the right thing to do. And I had to thank God for her listening to me. Officer Green just starred at Kalaya and me.

"Mr. Davis."

What is it this time Officer? You've heard what the lady said." I took a long deep breath because my voice started louder and didn't feel like getting arrested for yelling or any kind of BS. "Look, Mr. Davis, all I was going to say was sorry because I was suspicious that you were wrong." Officer Green said as he and Trisha left to go fill out a police report.

The Moment Kalaya and I went back inside my apartment I thought we'd continue where we left off, but I was dead wrong. Kalaya had her jacket and everything else she brought with her. Including this new Oil fragrance of hers called lich me all over. I jumped in front of her trying to make eye contact. I wanted to explain this is not how I wanted our night to be. "Kalaya you have to listen to me this is just a misunderstanding."

"Get off me keep your fucking hands off me."

I kept trying to calm Kalaya down until Wham. Kalaya slapped me across the face. "Chris when you get those skeletons out of your closet you let me know."

Kalaya kept pointing her finger in my face. "I'm tired of being the other woman with every man I get involved with."

Kalaya exhaled I could tell she was hurt by Trisha showing up at my house.

"I was ready to give you everything Chris even Shaq up with your ass. How could you do this shit too me Chris?" "Look it wasn't my fault! Now if you let me…"

Kalaya quickly put her hand on my face. "Look, Chris, I'm not one of your little girlfriends I'm a grown woman and I deserve to be treated like one."

I knew better than to argue with a woman especially when their upset. I watched

Kalaya walked out my apartment. I remember my boy Daniel telling me everything happens for a reason. It's bad because I really think we could have had something.

The court house was huge as usual was huge as usual.

"Ladies and Gentlemen of the Jury we are here today to present to you all the evidence that my client Mr. Chris Davis not responsible for the death of Ms. Kim Williams."

All eyes were on me and Katrina and from the way things were going I knew this nightmare would be over. I was surprised to see Katrina's parents and friends there to support me or maybe they just came to see her in action.

"Ms. Williams may you call your first witness." The Judge asked.

Katrina touched my shoulder whispering... "It'll be alright let's just deal with this now."

"Thank you, honor! My first witness is Jennifer Wilson to the stand."

I watched Jennifer go to the stand as she placed her left hand on the bible as the Court Officer asked her. "Do you swear to tell the truth the whole truth and nothing but the truth to help you, God?"

"I do."

"Ms. Wilson, would you please tell the court why you are here in this courtroom today?"

"Yes! Because a friend of mine was arrested for a crime."

"Jennifer turned around and looked at the Judge. Your Honor, I had no idea she committed any crime at all."

"Ms. Williams before your friend China was arrested what was it you two planned on doing at this club you all were at?"

"You know the usual thing we do at clubs. Dance, drink, flirt with men especially when they're drunk."

"Why is that, Ms. Wilson?"

A smile came across Ms. Wilson's face. "Well that's the best time to get in a man's pockets and get them to buy you drinks but that night arrested. China was on some next shit."

"I will not have that kind of language in my courtroom, Ms. Wilson."

Ms. Wilson turned her head to face the Judge. "Sorry, your honor but you've got to, believe me, I had no idea China wanted us too robe anyone."

"No further question your honor!"

I watched Katrina walk back to the desk looking confident.

"Ms. Wilson, what is your relationship with Chin?"

"Well, we had recently got engaged."

I watched Jennifer wipe her face as tears started dripping from her eyes.

Ms. Dutch screamed at Ms. Wilson without even giving her time to exhale. "Ok! Let's try this again. Ms. Wilson, would you please tell the court what was your relationship with China?"

"Yes! I have nothing to be ashamed of. Before this incident happened China and I had recently got engaged."

"What? Get the fuck out of here." One of the Jury's said.

More tears came down Jennifer's face. "Yes! Your honor, it is true, but I recently found out how much of a bully China is. But it's true we planned on getting married once we found out gay marriage was allowed in some states."

Objection your honor! We're not here to talk about the witness's sexual relationship. We're here to prove a man's innocence."

Sustained. The Judge said shaking his head. I guess the Judge was just as surprised as everyone in the court was to here that statement.

"Do have any further questions, Ms. Dutch?"

Yes, I do your honor because Mr. Williams over there what's the persecution to believe he's innocent. And as I stated the first time we were here in this courtroom justice must be served.

"Ms. Dutch just ask the question." The Judge said.

Not a problem your honor. Ms. Wilson, I recall you saying that you and China intended to get into a couple of men's pockets while they were drunk or by putting drugs in their drinks why is that."

"You're a woman you should know there is no romance without a fiancé but these last couple of weeks I've learned that it can't always be about getting into a man's pockets or what that man can do for you."

"Objection your honor what does this have to do with the case?"

"Sustained."

"Fine no further questions your honor."

"Ms. Wilson you my step down."

One hour later the Judge finally came out to tell the court his decision.

He sentenced China 25 to life in prison with a quarter of a million dollars bail. As for Jennifer, she was sentenced to a year of counseling. The Judge let the court know that all charges against me were dropped Katrina started jumping up and down like she had just won the lotto. I don't know which was more important to Kalaya proving my innocence or winning the case.

Before we all left the court Jennifer came up to me telling me China might be pregnant by me.

Damn, this was not the news I needed to here to start a celebration.

25

Stephan

Whoever said it would be tough when you get married knew what they were talking about. "Stephan I don't feel like having sex right now I'm just too tired."

Too tired, too tired. That's all I've been hearing for the last two months.

Now me being the young Mack that I was I kept my cool. I simply placed my hand on one of Stacy's thighs and was about to put two fingers inside her womanhood just to get her in the mood. She started moaning and quickly put a stop to it.

"Look, Stephan, what part of not in the mood don't you understand."

I quickly jumped out of my bed in frustration and headed to the kitchen.

"Stephan gets back in this damn bed," Stacy shouted out.

When I opened the refrigerator door I quickly poured myself a cup of Raspberry Smirnoff.

'Too tired, too tired. Damn, Stacy had said those words to me so much that it stock in my damn head.'

"Stephan, why the hell are you drinking this time of night have you lost your mind?"

I didn't need this aggravation shit! I should've just stayed in the Studio. Instead, I wanted to be with my wife. I just looked at her and took another sip of my drink.

"Answer me, Stephan, why are drinking this late at night?"

"Because I'm a grown man, and I can't get sex from my damn wife! Stacy, I've been patient enough with you. Look I could understand a few weeks before we were married, but that was months ago."

"Is that all you think about is sex, Stephan? So now it's just because I'm your wife I'm supposed to give you what you want."

"We're fucking married for God sacks Stacy have you ever heard of the word satisfaction."

"And have you ever heard of being too tired?" Stacy paused and gave me one of her Venom looks.

"Stephan we've been married for only 3 and a half months and if this is how you're going to act when we have our children you'd better change now."

I just shook my head and started smiling as I was headed back to the bedroom I heard the phone ring and Stacy quickly went to answer it.

"Who the fuck is calling my damn house this late in the morning?"

"Stephan baby this is a business call please let's not fight anymore."

I just looked at her and then threw on some sweet paints on a stormed out the door I was too pissed to even look at Stacy.

"Stephan, where are you going?"

 I heard people talk about sex slowing down after children were born, but both Stacy and I didn't have any children. For Christ shake we we're both in our mid-twenties

What the hell could she be tired of? I just jumped in my Nissan Altima 3.5 and acted as if I was driving off.

I threw on Usher's CD confession. Before Stacy and I we're married we would always find time to make sweet love.

Stacy would always tell me that she'd never feel down and that I always gave her strength when she was with me.

Even our Honeymoon was a wired one. Although we were interment that night Stacy just wasn't herself. She only had a cup of wine while I drank 4 cups.

Yes, people, this was our Honeymoon. Our intimacy only lasted for about 30 minutes. Because Stacy feel asleep shit for that whack of sex I could have gotten I could have gotten some from an ex of mine or one of my old hoes, but instead, I just laid in bed next to Stacy and held her in my arms.

As I sat there reminiscing on my boring honeymoon. I knew it was time for a change but before I could even think about before I could even it a cab pulled in front of my building blowing its horn.

'Damn doesn't this Nigga realize people are sleeping.' I said to myself.

"What the fuck?"

"Stacy?"

I watched Stacy get in the cab although she didn't look too happy about getting in. I had some questions that needed answering. '1 where could she be going? 2 Why didn't she tell me about where she was going? Especially if she was so damn tired 3 what could she be hiding that she didn't want me to find out?'

Minutes later after following the cab, Stacy was in for nearly 45 minutes. 'I'm too tired Stephan I'm too tired that all could keep picture Stacy saying.'

I watched her walk inside a club called Sin City. Believe it or not people my wife

looked real relieved to be at this Sin City stripe club.

My eyes were wide open when I saw a man escorting Stacy inside. 'How foul is this?'

As I walked inside there were women on stage dancing freaky and some were even rubbing up on guys while collecting money.

One walked up to me, but I rejected her immediately because I quickly got a vibe of what kind of women were in this club. The bad thing about it is that I was getting the feeling my wife was one of them.

One hour later after having my second long island ice tea. There was no more of me holding my head down I watched each woman do their solo performance. One by one each stripper was either on a pole doing their thing or out there just flirting with the men in the club. One woman walked up to me dancing to R-Kelly I'm a flirt song. She had on red G-strings and a thrown bra trying to lead me on. She didn't know I already knew the game. "What's wrong lover boy don't you want this?" She said while dancing in front of me and doing tricks with her tongue.

I handed her $10 and told her to keep it moving. "No mother fucker I'm going to make you want this pussy here." Let's head to the VIP room she said while showing me her left nipple. "Look Ms. I 'm a married man and I'll hit you off with another $10 if Stacy is here?"

"Well, there's only one Stacy here that I know and she's the white bitch."

A huge smile came across her face when I mentioned money. She quickly told me Stacy was in the back room with their boss Baby Cream and that she was on stage next to doing her solo performance.

As soon as they called Stacy's name I just couldn't believe what I was seeing.

While all these horny Nigga's were busy watching my wife get in their pockets. I sat there thinking one of the things a faithful husband could find out is that his wife has been stripping behind his back.

Although I didn't freak out this was still a life lesson for me. As a husband, I had felt all kinds of mixed emotions. Like what if she's been fucking some of these Nigga's in this club's VIP room, and what if she's been fucking some of these horny Nigga's raw.

I noticed Stacy was looking like she was a professional pleasing the crowd.

Now as a Mack, I knew my cool was to just observe. I watched Stacy while one man kept putting money out on stage. I still couldn't believe what I was seeing my wife working in a strip club and I know nothing about this.

As I drove home I had a big surprise waiting at home Stacy. The only thing was this might be the hardest thing I've ever done.

It was close to 6:00 a.m. when Stacy walked through the door. My eyes quickly locked on to her as I got up from our couch.

I didn't say a word to Stacy instead I gave a vicious look. As I walked in front of her I quickly grabbed her by the arm with my teeth clenched together. "Why didn't you tell me?"

"Tell you what? Baby, you're hurting me."

I let go of her arm and pushed her down to the couch. "Stephan, what the hell is your problem?"

"You've been stripping behind my back. You've been lying to me all this time.

In fact, everything about you is a lie, right? I see why you've been too tired to have sex with me you've been fucking all those men you bring into that VIP room."

Stephan, please. You don't know what you're talking about."

"So you're telling me you haven't been stripping? So you're telling me you haven't been shacking your ass in front of a bunch of horny Niggas?"

"No, what I'm saying to you is I've been working and I haven't committed any kind of adultery. How could you even think that about me."

I could tell Stacy was hurt, more hurt than she couldn't ever imagined I didn't give a damn about her feelings.

"How long has this been going on? And why the hell didn't you tell me about this so-called job?"

Tears started coming down her face. "I was going to Stephan. Believe me, Stephan, there were so many times I wanted too but...but."

"But you just couldn't wait to have all that dick inside you right?"

Wham! Stacy slapped me across the face. "Now Stephan I'm you're fucking wife. You have no idea what the hell I've been through going through these past few months. Working at Sin City has helped me pay my bills and I needed the money."

I don't believe this shit I'm married to a fucking stripper. I've been doing all the right things with the wrong woman. You're telling me you couldn't get a regular 9-5 job."

"No, I couldn't damn it. For the last time, no jobs were hiring I've applied at just about every job you could think about." Stacy had tears coming down even more than before. Damn it, Stephan, why do you have animosity towards strippers? You have no idea what they go through."

I just looked at her shaking my head. The truth is I was embarrassed to call her my wife. "I've heard enough because next thing you know you'll be bringing some type of disease... Stacy get the hell out of here."

Excuse me mother fucker! This is my fucking crib, I've been paying rent and bills here before I even met your ass. If anyone is going to get out of here it's you."

Stacy didn't have to say another word. I just left the house slamming the door behind me. If there was one big lesson I've learned from all of this was that my wife was thinking of herself when it came to her stripping. It was time to think of me and do me first.

26

Hassan

It was a little over 8:00 pm Katrina and I were headed to her parent's house.

They invited us for Sunday dinner and today we were going to announce our engagement and Katrina's three-month pregnancy.

I kept reminding her to take it easy this was going to be our first child and I didn't what her feeling like she was under pressure telling her folks the news. It was this announcement that kept stressing her out because of the way her parents felt about me. Let's face it people if Katrina and I were to be a married couple and new parents I knew sooner or later I'd have to deal with her parents.

30 minutes later we were at Katrina's parent's house having Sunday dinner. Unfortunately, there were family members there even Katrina didn't expect to see including her cousin.

"So Hassan how's your friend Chris doing these days since his innocence has been proven." Katrina's father asked.

"Well from what I know he's been doing fine," I said while staring at him.

"So when's that non-profit recreation center of yours opening up Hassan?"

I felt like clenching my fist and just going off on this man for trying to embarrass me. I kept my cool and told Katrina's family the truth. I was determined to show Katrina's father that I deserved her love and hand in marriage. Well, Mr. Williams, It's still in process and…"

Before I could say another word Katrina stood up looking at everyone at the table. Her Aunt Regina her Cousin Nicole and her man Darrin who was Katrina's ex-man. I glanced at her while she kept squeezing my hand and keeping eye contact with everyone at the table. "Yes, Daddy Hassan recreation is still in process and you and mommy might even see you're grandchild."

"Or children!" I said.

"Or Children," Katrina said while holding her belly.

"What is this my baby is expecting?"

"Yes, mom Hassan and I are expecting our first child in about another 6 months."

"What? Princess, you've been pregnant for three months and we knew nothing about this?" Katrina's father asked while staring at me.

The way Katrina's father kept staring at me made me think. Here was a man who swore I was no good for his daughter. Since day one he thought either I was too trifling too ghetto or didn't have the right jo to support his daughter. Yes, I was from the hood and still had that hood mentality in me but he had no idea the bond his daughter and I share. Katrina's father and I stared at each other for a few seconds and with our eyes locked on each other, I knew things were going to get nasty in Katrina's parent's house.

"How do plan on raising this baby you are expecting You expecting my daughter to bring to this world, Hassan?"

"Daddy!" Katrina shouted out looking as though she was ready to Snape on her father.

"Sorry Princess but…"

"But nothing James can't you see our daughter's in love and Hassan seems to be the very decent man for our daughter."

"Thanks, mother but me being pregnant isn't the only announcement Hassan and I have to make." Suddenly Katrina stood up holding her belly as she took a glance at everyone at the table.

Man, I was praying this announcement wouldn't upset anyone in here or start a brawl but I remember what Chris said to me the last time we talked. 'Chris just be a man about it.'

"Baby let me announce this one. Mr. and Mrs. Williams your daughter who's my fiancé have been engaged for the past 4 months now."

"Oh, really that's great because Darrin and I are looking for a couple to chill out with." Katrina's cousin said.

"Well keep looking." Katrina said.

"Wait, Fiancé?" Katrina's father quickly snapped. "This is all going way too fast princess don't you have a career to think about?"

The way Katrina's father was looking he wasn't even trying to hold his composure. He even brought up the time he caught me kissing that teenager.

Mrs. Williams quickly had a surprised look on her face but obliviously they had no idea that Katrina and I had gotten past that. Our announcement surprised Katrina's whole family, especially he father. "Hassan." I was sure Katrina's father was going to say something smart out of his mouth again but Katrina cut him off immediately.

"Damn it, Dad! Why do insist on torturing us? Can't you just be happy for us? We're going to have a happy and healthy marriage just like you and mom." Katrina said staring at her father and everyone else at the table.

'You go girl.' Now fellas that's when you know you've got a good woman.

Relax Princess no one here is torturing you two. And I want you to remember who you raising your voice too because like it or not we're still you're parents. I've come to realize that Hassan is a good man and he's proven it."

Everyone was silent as Mr. Williams continued to say... "Hassan you've got to understand the hardest thing for a man is to watch his daughter grow up to be in the arms of another man. Especially if she's been treated badly in the past."

Katrina's father glanced at Darrin then looked right back at me smiling.

I kept trying to read his expression but I couldn't quit read it. He extended his hand to me. "Hassan welcome to the family and I'd be honored to give my daughter away. If this is really what you two want, you'd better be good to her because that's our only daughter." Her father said.

I felt relieved to hear those words and suddenly the tension between us quickly faded away. Not only had our announcement shocked everyone but my parents had finally accepted Hassan for who he is and what he does for a living.

I saw Katrina's cousin glaring at her like she was jealous and why not? I had what most brothers would want a good woman with a good career who was about to become a parent and a wife now that was something beautiful.

I kissed my future mother-in-law and shook her husband's hand. I also kissed Katrina's aunt on her cheek and let them all know I appreciated their support. There's nothing like having the support of your family and friends. I was truly in love with Hassan. Sure the sex between us was great but love meant more than that to us. That's something Katrina brought back into my life and to this day I thank God for bringing her into my life.

Later that evening "Katrina." I said whispering in her ear.

There I was lying in the bed with Katrina next to me rubbing my back we were both naked and discussing things that lovers do. As I leaned on top of her our lips quickly connected. "Baby I want you to know I'm going too always be doing right by you and the baby."

"Hassan I already know that. Now make love too me."

"As you wish my queen but I still intend to make your body dance with my tongue."

"Uhhh." Katrina moaned because it felt like I was already inside her. I took it easy putting my manhood inside her as she wrapped her arms around me holding me tight. I love you." We both said to each other as our tongues united with each other.

Several hours later I was lying down holding Katrina in my arms. I had a huge smile on my face not just because of the passionate love we just made but as I laid down thinking about Katrina and myself of how lucky I was.

Katrina could have easily walked out on me when the teenager kissed me.

After accepting my apology and understanding why did what she did. I can honestly say I have a great woman in my life and I can't wait until she becomes my wife.

27

Katrina

One month later. "Are you nervous?" My mom asked.

In a way I was, but I didn't want to ruin my makeup so I tried my best to hold back my tears. I was nervous just because over the years I had seen people who were in love and get married end up in divorce. Wither it was people from church or people that I knew I concluded that marriage isn't honored like it used to be. "Katrina."

"Katrina!" Kalaya shouted.

"Girl I never seen anyone day dream on their wedding day." Rose said.

"You aren't having second thoughts are you Katrina?" Stacy asked.

"No you'll I'm not having second thoughts at all and no I'm not nervous. I just want everything to go smoothly."

"Well then get you dressed because it's show time."

"Yes, mom." I gestured for Kalaya to help me zip my dress up. Stacy and Rose went down stairs.

"You know girl I hope you and Hassan have a really good marriage because I think you two are perfect for each other."

"Thanks a lot, girl but you know you and Chris are next."

Kalaya cracked a smile.

"That would be nice but in reality, I think Rose and Kenny are next."

It doesn't matter who's getting married next! My mother shouted.

"What does matter is that you and that soon to be son in law of mine make it down that aisle.

Now you've got about 5 to ten minutes to meet Hassan at the altar Kalaya let's go down stairs."

"Oh no, I don't need this." The Moment my Mother opened the door I felt a migraine coming on. My mom was huffing and puffing like she was ready to pull a Media with a couple of combinations.

"Please, I'm not here to case any trouble."

"You damn right you're not here too cause any trouble! Not you or anyone else will ruin my baby's big day."

I had no idea why Darrin was here or how he got inside. 'God please don't let him ruin the biggest day of my life.'

You're got some nerve coming here Darrin." Kalaya said pointing her fingers in Darrin's face.

"And you've got some nerve getting in my face when you and Katrina no how I get down. Darrin said glaring at Kalaya and then my mother.

"Darrin I don't care how thuggish you think you are you're not going to ruin the biggest day of my life."

"Wow! Wow! Slow down please I'm not here too cause any trouble."

"You damn right you're not, and you'd better be happy we're in c church because I'd make you pay for every putting your hands on my daughter."

I quickly noticed the facial expression on my mother's face. She was ready to go off on Darrin.

I gave her and Kalaya her and Kalaya a pleading look letting them know I had everything under control. Although I was a little nervous I still stepped in his face asking what he wanted and why was he at my Wedding uninvited.

"Look, Katrina, like I said I'm not here to cause any trouble, and here's your wedding present." Darrin said as he left giving my mother and Kalaya as stare.

I opened Darrin's present as soon as Kalaya and my mom left. I was real curious about Darrin's so-called present.

It was a wedding card with a note and a man holding a woman in his arms. I quickly read the note called I should have. 'Hey, Katrina baby first and foremost I'd like to congratulate you.

Although I feel like I should have been the one marrying you we all know I messed up big time. I want you to remember something; something that you'll cherish for the rest of your life. Remember the passionate kisses we shared. Remember the pleasurable things I've done when all I wanted was for you to have fun? Katrina, you know how people say you don't miss a good thing until it's gone well they were right. Because if I had been the kind of man you needed and I'm talking about the kind that women like yourself want and need in your life. The kind that respects you and shows you how much he appreciates you in his life most people just don't appreciate a good thing until it's gone.

I should have been the kind of man who walked the walk with you in the rain and held your hand in front of his family and friends. I should have been the man massaging you're feet and washing your hair. Let's face it Katrina you were that special woman in my life and some men like myself take women like you for granted. So my advice to that Nigga you're about to marry is the way you start a relationship is the way you should continue it. Congratulations again. I'll take good care of your cousin.' Love Darrin.

It's funny how it took me to get married for Darrin to finally admit he had a good thing and let it slip away. Don't get me wrong people I may not be the prettiest woman on earth, especially in my condition but I damn sure would be the happiest because after I walk the ale and say those two words that some people dream of hearing I would now be known as Mr. Hassan Powell.

As my Father walked down the ale with me I noticed that the church was packed. There were at least 300 guests in attendance including that bitch ass cousin of mine Tina.

When the music was playing Hassan his best man Chris and the pastor were already down the aisle. Even my three brides maid Kalaya Rose and Stacy were down there. They were already escorted by the groomsmen.

The cameras kept clicking as daddy continued to take that walk with me down the ale. I tried my best to hold back my tears but wasn't successful after daddy finished walking me I looked at Hassan and could tell he wanted to cry too.

"I love you." Hassan whispered to me.

I quickly whispered right back to him because in a matter of moments, I would be his African-American Queen and he'd be my King.

'Thank you, God. Because right now I feel like the luckiest woman in the world.'

28
Kalaya

Cameras were clicking everywhere at the wedding party as the guests took several pictures. We all looked great as we stood there in our braid maid white dresses.

I know there were a few guests that were stunned to see Stacy there. After all, she was the only white girl that was in the wedding and at the party but it didn't seem to matter much because the men that were taking pictures just overlooked her complexion and kept the cameras going. I had to give Katrina and Hasan their props. Although they were expecting a baby they both went all out spending 30,000 on their wedding to make sure everything was just the way they wanted it to be. Katrina's dress alone was nearly 10,000 it was a white Vera Wang dress. It was one in a million because it was custom-made. Our dresses were similar to Katrina's and as Katrina and Hassan made their way to the dance floor the song the DJ threw on Brain McKnight's song 'Back at one.'

I was very happy for Katrina and Hassan to meet each other at the Altar.

As the next song came on everyone grabbed a partner and danced to Luther Van dross 'If this world were mine.'

Now usually at Weddings, the groom dances with the braid maids but this was different Rose was I the arms of her man Kenny. I had to give Stacy her props even though her and Stephen's marriage didn't work out and he brought his own date she still didn't let that bother her. Although I didn't like her date who was her boss Babe Cream.

I knew it wasn't right to judge others so I just stood there and watched and as I shook my head I mean both Stacy and Stephen were acting like they never made vows to one another. I guest too some people love is just a word but again who was I to judge?

Five minutes late I was having a glass of E and J with the girls. "Katrina congratulations again girl we all wish the best for you and Hassan. I said.

Before Rose and Stacy could say anything this tall muscular-skinned man came up to me asking to dance I just turned to my girls and quickly shook my head no.

'Damn, I enjoyed turning him down because I'd usually dance with the first man that would ask me to dance.'

Rose shoved me saying… "Girl what's wrong with you Kalaya it's your turn to be happy and find your Romeo and you won't find him by turning guy's down."

"Rose he only asked her to dance. Katrina said.

"Look my point is she can't keep letting past relationships stop her from being happy and finding her a good man."

That's so easy for you to say, Rose. You'll already have men in your lives that care about you."

'The nerve of her as if she knew me like that, but she was right I have been letting my past stop me from finding a do-right man.'

As I watched Katrina Rose and Stacy head to the dance floor I thought about what Rose had said. It really would be nice to have a good man of mine lying in bed next to me every night. But I refuse to be degraded or humiliated by being some man's mistress or part-time lover.

Moments later after listening to a few Luther Van Dross songs. 'Always and forever.' The next song the DJ threw on was dance with my father. "May I have this dance?' Chris came up to me and asked.

I started having flash backs of the lustful experience I went through with this man.

Will I have to deal with the same embarrassment if I allow this man to get close to me? Sure it would be just a dance but I was not about to let him have the best of both worlds at least not with me anyway.

"I think you need to be dancing with your date, Chris."

He just smiled. "Kalaya I can't blame you for being upset at me. Our relationship ended before it even started and I apologize for that. Look I'm a man of God and I can't control how you or most of these other women may feel about me. Now all I'm asking for is a dance."

"Fine."

I extended my hand out to him as he led me to the dance floor. I saw how his date Ms. Trisha looked at me in her black dress I just rolled my eyes at her.

"Isn't this a lovely song Kalaya? And by the way, you look fabulous in that dress."

I quickly cracked a smile telling Chris thank you. Chris knew me well enough to know that one line wouldn't get in my panties.

After a few minutes of dancing, I was beginning to feel relaxed. As Brain McKnight's song ended Trisha came and took Chris by the hand telling him their song was next.

"Wait Trisha can't you see I was in the middle of something? It's not always about you."

"Relax Chris I understand. Trisha Chris is your man and I know you want to enjoy yourself with him."

"You got that right."

Hood Lover

"You know Trisha I'm trying to be nice here but don't think I won't kick your little ass in here."

 Chris jumped in front of us as soon as our fists were ready to start flying at one another. "Ladies this is not the time or place for cat fighting. Now if you'll still want to have your cat fight go on ahead just don't do it in here or around me."

I exhaled and opened my eyes knowing that Chris was right. This was not the time or place for me to turn She-Hulk in here, besides I wanted to show Miss Trisha who the better woman was.

"Look Kalaya again I'm sorry about how things turned out between us."

"Chris you've said enough. My heart can't take any more of this male bullshit.

I've had it with men like you taking advantage of women like myself."

Chris shook his head and started smiling. "Kalaya you're confused and you confusing lust with love. Look let me introduce you to my boy Daniel I think you two might hit it off."

"Excuse me, Chris? Just who the hell do you think I am?" I said with my arms folded.

Chris walked up to me as if he was ready to take my breath away but his facial expression said what was really on his mind. "Look Kalaya I don't blame you for being defensive but I am letting you know I have a friend who just might be right for you."

"Whatever Chris thanks, but no thanks look I'm just hoping your little girlfriend Trisha knows how to hold on to her man."

I wasn't proud of the way I handed that situation. But I didn't seem to care I didn't even care about them missing their song. But what I did care about was Chris respecting me. 'Ladies you all know the respect we demand in this era right?'

As I came out of the ladies' room Rose came up too me asking if was everything alright. I told her it wasn't anything I couldn't handle and I let her know what was going on and why I'd never mess with one of Chris's friends.

"Sweetie, what did we discuss earlier?"

"Rose think about it messing with one of Chris's friends would be like dancing with the Devil."

"Honey, you don't even know him. Why are you judging the brother already?"

"That's exactly my point I don't want to get to know the Devil and Chris's friend is just out to get some."

"Have you even met this guy? He could be just right for you. Your just too angry right now to get to know the man right now."

Rose was right I was upset the look on my face said it all. This excruciating pain in my heart I was feeling had reminded me that all this time the man I was feeling was already in love with another woman.

"Excuse me but can I have this next dance with you before you and your girlfriend hit the dance floor?" This tall brown-skinned man asked me.

He stood about 6 feet with a nice short haircut. He had a nice Steve Harvey suit on. The same one I was going to get Chris.

"Excuse me but she's not my girlfriend. We're women who love the real thing not some fucking toy."

"My fault Kalaya I didn't mean to offend you or your friend here. Now all."

"Wait! Wait! Wait! How do you even know her name? What are you a stalker or something?" Rose asked.

"Again I want to apologize to both of you my name is Daniel and it was Chris who pointed me out to you."

"Come on Kalaya he's only asking for a dance." Rose said smiling.

"Ok, Ladies, it's time for these last two special songs." The DJ said.

"Oh, this is my song." Daniel said.

'I might as well go with the flow one little dance can't hurt.'

Within seconds Daniel took my hand and together we were on the dance floor for what seemed like hours.

After a few minutes of dancing, I was feeling so relaxed. I laid my head on Daniel's shoulder and just closed my eyes. I was in another world no one else surrounding us mattered to me anymore.

"So how's life been treating you? Daniel asked.

Damn, some men can ruin the moment. "You don't want me to answer that especially the way you men treat women you make it feel as though love is pain and headaches."

"I'm sorry to hear that, but in this era, we're living in you can't blame men for what they do."

"And what's that supposed to mean?"

"Think about it in this era we're in it's the men who are getting hurt by women. Especially if she's with another woman that can mess with a man's ego."

I quickly stopped dancing and folded my arms asking... "Is that the real reason you men are never satisfied with one woman, because of your egos?"

"Look Kalaya, I can go on and on as to why men cheat, but right now I'd just like to continue dancing before the song goes off."

I had to give him his props Daniel wasn't a bad dancer and he was very flexible we continued to dance to R Kelly's you saved me song.

Daniel explained to me that men hurt too. "Kalaya sometimes men hurt even more than women especially if he's feeling that woman."

This was interesting although I didn't believe a word he was saying I still wanted to hear what he had to say.

We both walked off the dance floor and sat at the table near the dance floor. For the next few minutes, the two of us sat at the table talking.

I let Daniel know I was real jaded about love and relationships he put his right hand fingers and palms so they could connect with mine. I cracked a smile after hearing what Daniel had to say. "Don't give up on love Kalaya. Yes, you have your reasons to be upset with men, but don't judge me because of the other men form your past."

Moments later everyone was at the table having dinner. We all made a toss to Hassan and Katrina's wedding. First, it was Stacy who spoke…

"Katrina I wish the very best for you and Hassan. May you both cherish each other's love as you grow old together and may God bless you both."

Next was Rose… "Katrina and Hassan you both deserve the best. And with a baby on the way you two will have time to rest."

Now it was my turn to say my poem I know my mind should be on this ceremony but it wasn't because the words Daniel was saying had brought orgasmic tingles to my

body. I was fantasying about Daniel, but as I noticed everyone's eyes were on me waiting to hear what I had to say I quickly stood up and dripped my poem.

"To Hassan and Katrina seeing the two of you walk down the aisle, you two have proven that love still does exist because when most men fall in love with us women hear those words we can't resist so again to the both of you congratulations cheers."

As everyone sat at the table having dinner Daniel and I went outside. He showed me the car he rented which was a Chrysler 300 I loved the fact that Daniel was honest with me about renting the car and not fronting like it was his. Because a lot of men these days are driving cars they know they can't afford.

"Daniel quickly started to massage my back. Thanks, Daniel this is just what I needed."

"That's the goal."

"Oh really? And just what is this goal of yours."

Daniel looked into my face saying... "My goal is to take your mind and body places it's never been before."

Without hesitating our tongues were exploring each other's. My eyes were completely closed and we kept kissing each other deeply and tenderly. Daniel started wrapping his arms around me as I caressed him.

Once our lips untangled from each other I started unbuttoning Daniel's shirt getting a good look at his brown-skinned muscular body. I removed Daniel's shirt and I could tell he was turned on by my actions. I started hugging Daniel because this might be the man God has sent to me to make my life complete.

"I want you." He said to me.

"I want you too." I replied.

My eyes traveled down to Daniel's waist and I unbuttoned his pants getting a look at his penis.

"Wait Kalaya there'll be times for us to taste each other."

"Well, Daniel your right, and as of right I want you to fuck me."

Daniel's hands were stroking through my hair while fucking me real hard and the way Daniel came had me oohing and ahhing. He watched me lick my lips and I'm sure he knew the sex we just had was a pleasure. "Don't think we're finished Kalaya I want you to get yours as well."

"Daniel, we've got to get back to the ceremony."

In a minute baby but right now I'm going to make your body real hot. I'm talking about to the point where you're body's craving for more."

"Ha, ha, and how's that?" I asked as I continued to laugh.

Daniel quickly put me on his lap and told me to keep as look out for people but I couldn't. I was riding his dick to fast and as I was Cumming my moans were getting louder and louder. For a moment I didn't care who heard my moaning that's when I knew it was time to stop and get back to the ceremony we laughed and giggled for the next ten minutes. So what is it you do for a living Daniel? I asked as he was zipping his paints and buttoning his shirt.

"It's funny you should ask that. I'm surprised Chris didn't tell you but I'm glad he didn't because he knows I don't like strangers in my business."

"Well, that's understandable."

I'll be starting my own magazine company called Black Love Entertainment. We'll be on newsstands soon.

In fact, I'll be in Baltimore next week discussing things with my editor."

"And how will you make time for me?" I asked with a look that let him know I demanded an answer.

"I don't know yet we can discuss it after the ceremony."

No, we'll discuss it now because had I known you were going to be the busy type instead of working a regular 9-5 and spending time with me on occasion I would've never had sex with you."

"I'm sorry you feel that way Kalaya but this is one part of what my magazine covers. How some people lust for love because they're confused about what love is."

"Excuse me!" I said as I boiled my fists ready to throw a punch at this man. But I could never let this dress get ruined. How could this happen to me I finally met a good man and it's still not working out for me.

As we were headed back to the ceremony I knew it was time for a change because no longer would I ever get hurt by another man.

29
Stacy

Then I was on my way to Court thinking one of the most painful things we women go through in life is a Divorce. I know in my heart I did everything in my heart to make my marriage work. I wanted to be the one to have Stephen's baby, although we had no children I still felt the pain other women go through when their families are being broken up my heart goes out to them.

I could never forget how I felt the day I received those divorce papers in the mail.

It was less than three weeks ago when my boss Babe Cream and I came from Katrina and Hassan's Wedding and Reception. "I can't believe this." I said as I opened the envelope.

Babe Cream could see the disappointed look I had on my face but I was also angry with Stephen for bringing that chick to the Reception with him. Chick is a word we women use when we're angry or jealous of other women. Kalaya and Rose felt I was weak for not approaching Stephen about that piece of trash he was with but I was not about to cause a seen at Katrina's wedding reception.

Babe Cream kept letting me know everything would be alright and that everything should be left in God's hands.

I remember it so well because I quickly changed the subject with him.

"You know Cream it's nice that you're here because I need to be held by a good friend."

I may be your boss Stacy but I'm always here if you need me."

"That's not what I meant. You know forget it because I even think you can move those hips right anyway. I shouted out.

"Excuse me?"

"You heard me I'm fucking angry plus I'm horny as hell this evening and…"

Before I could say another word Babe Cream, put his hand over my mouth saying… "Don't be coming down on me because of your problems. Now what you need to do is catch your breath."

Before I could even expect hale Cream's tongue was in my mouth. Cream kept palming my ass as we kept exploring each other with French kisses.

'Damn, this man can kiss.'

The way Babe Cream, kept kissing my lips and neck really and had my juices flowing. I wanted Cream, inside of me after those soft kisses he kept planting on me. I knew this was something we didn't plan to happen because I was not about to be one of Cream's hoes. The way he smiled at me made me feel as though I already was.

"Hey, Stacy relax! I know seeing your Husband with another woman was a shack but since we already know each other mentally it is time for us to know each other physically and orally. So let me make your body real hot the way you and most women dreamed of."

Cream and I started undressing each other slowly. He let me know how much he admired my body and as Cream unbuttoned my bra his tongue quickly traced down each one of my nipples.

From my chest to my belly button Cream's tongue had my whole body shivering.

Before I could say a word he had my legs spread wide open and with his tongue doing all kinds of tricks to my clit all I could say was. 'Damnnnnnn.'

That felt so good Cream's tongue was very thick and it made my moans because louder the moment he started sucking my vagina.

15 minutes later Cream turned me around and had one of my ass cheeks in the palm of his hand.

"Look how lovely your ass cheeks are Stacy." Cream said while rubbing my cheeks.

"Just put that dick of yours inside me Cream."

Cream didn't hesitate at all and the position we were in gave him total access and control of how things would be going down.

After a few moans of pleasure, I was almost ready to cum. Cream knew I was ready to cum, but h immediately put me in the doggy-style position. The cream kept going faster and faster and faster until my legs started shaking. Cream, quickly held my waist tighter and started moving slowly as I screamed out.

"This is the best pussy you've ever had."

Babe Cream started smacking my ass cheeks.

"Yeah, that's the way to do it, baby." 'This is what I needed some good dick to take my mind off what was to come.'

Moments later my body was drained I collapsed and I just fell asleep.

Once the Court Officers told everyone in the courtroom to sit down I knew this was it.

There would be no turning back. There would be no turning back. There would be no chance for Stephen and I to work things out.

As Judge Perkins made her appearance I looked across the room hoping to catch eye contact hoping to catch eye contact with Stephan, but his eyes were focused on the Judge and what she was saying.

Ladies and Gentlemen, here we have a Divorce case of Mr. Stephen Davis vs. Ms. Stacy Hope. Stephen, you're filing for divorce because you accused your wife of being unfaithful and not honoring the marriage.

"And she's been lying to me before the marriage even started." Stephen shouted out.

Relax Mr. Stephen I'm not done yet. And don't ever interrupt me in my courtroom." The Judge said to Stephen.

"Now before I hear both of your stories I'd like to know have you two tried to make this marriage work?"

The Judge quickly gave us one of her lectures on young people getting married and divorced at an early age. She even mentioned some may be divorced within a year of their marriage because they don't understand the value of marriage.

"You should be lecturing her she's the one who needs it." Stephen shouted out.

"Mr. Stephen what I'm saying is for everyone in this courtroom to hear not just you and Ms. Hope. And I told you before not to interrupt me in my courtroom. Now another outburst like that again and I will have you removed.

One hour later as I was walking out of the courtroom I felt really bad because of the way things went with me Stephen it was nice that Cream was there to confrontment

Me but not even he could stop the tears dripping from my eyes.

The moment Babe Cream and I were outside I heard someone call my name. It was Stephen and as he walked up to me I didn't have anything to say. I just looked at him as he approached me with a big smile on his face. That told me he was happy to be a single man again.

"You no Stacy this could've been avoided if you were honest with me from the beginning. You brought this upon yourself but I have to admit what that Judge said earlier made sense."

"And what was that Stephen? She said a whole lot of things that made sense."

True that but what she said that got my attention was the same thing Judge Madame would say back when she was on divorce court. 'Look deep before you leap.'

"Goodbye, Stacy."

"Don't worry she's in good hands." Cream said while taking my hand as we started to work off. I dared Stephen to try to stop me, but I knew that Stephen didn't pay Babe Cream any attention being the Mack he was he always kept his cool. Although I was now a divorced woman I knew it was time to start a new life.

30
Katrina

"I love you, Mrs. Katrina Powell."

"I love you too Mr. Hassan Powell."

I love it when Hassan calls me his Mrs. Hassan and were lie down talking with each other for about 20 minutes. We had been at it for several hours earlier making love to one another like most newlyweds do.

"You no babe since I've met you I've become a better man and with you trusting me I became a man that you can trust and understand. Katrina, I just want you to know I'm blessed you've made me a Father and…"

Before Hassan could even finish my tongue was in his mouth. We started kissing passionately but Hassan broke the kiss. Babe unless you've got some Viagra Mr. Giant needs a rest."

I lay on top and smiled at Hassan. "Well, Mr. Giant better get back up because I'm ready to take him down again.

Within seconds Mr. Giant was up and Hassan immediately grabbed my heart-shaped ass giving it to me hard from the back. My moans always got Hassan excited and this time was no different because Hassan kept going faster as I kept pushing back against him.

"Oh yes… Yes, babe…Oh yes, Hassan give it to me faster…Oh…Faster."

"Waaaah…ahhh…waaa."

Hassan quickly pulled out of me and went to the bathroom to clean himself.

My daughter needed a diaper change and Hassan immediately took charge and took care of it.

Hassan had shown me over and over that, he was a good Husband and a great Father.

"Katrina?" Hassan quickly came back in bed putting his hand under my chin. Reminding me how he loved me.

"Hi, babe what time are your parents and everyone else coming over for dinner?"

" Oh shit! I completely forget about it." I quickly jumped in the shower.

I'm glad Hassan and I went food shopping the other day. I immediately went to the kitchen and started cooking.

30 Minutes later my parents came through the doorway.

Hassan handed my father his little granddaughter so he could bond with her while my Mother came into the kitchen to help me finish cooking. It never changed my Mother was still giving me directions on seasoning as if I was new to this.

Everyone was at the table ready to eat my Mother insisted on bringing the last plate of food to the table which was salad.

As my Mother sat down she looked at everyone at the table. "Chris will you do the honors and say grace for us please."

"Sure thing."

I couldn't believe this person my Mother was here giving orders like she was head of the household in my own home. But it was something I didn't mind at all.

Everyone bowed their heads as Chris said grace I like the fact that Chris got right to the point and ended it with a blissful Amen.

As we all lifted our heads I smiled at everyone sitting at the two tables. Stacy was now living a happy single life and was still working for that Babe Cream fellow and at that Sin City strip club, but who was I to Judge?

Kalaya told me earlier she was going to let love come to her naturally. Because she learned to keep feelings from sex I guess she now realizes that true love doesn't happen overnight. Rose and her man Kenny were living the life like Hassan and I.

Chris was the one person in the room we were all happy for because of the things he had been through and overcome. It was too bad that Chris and Kalaya couldn't get something started. Hassan and I had huge smiles on our faces watching our daughter's Godfather put his bible down feed her and then cuddle with her Chris has proven that you can be a Hood lover and still be a man of God.

Discussion and question

1. What do you think of Chris and how would've handle his situation.
2. Has this book changed the way you look at women and what some of them go through?
3. Who was your favorite character?
4. If you were Katrina would you have forgiven Stacy?
5. What do you think of Katrina's parents?
6. Would you stay with a person if you found out they worked in a strip club?
7. Did you feel any compassion for Kalaya and her wanting a man or herself?
8. How would you handle a woman like Rose?
9. What was your opinion of Stacy helping Kalaya?
10. On a scale of 1to 10, what would you give this book?

Coming Sept 2014

Based on the Comedy Stage Play Someone's gotta be on top

1

Shemar

Call me conceited, overconfident but there's nothing more that turns me on than Hearing a woman screen and moan pleasure. As I was making love to Crystal I held her hips going in and out of her as her legs were wrapped around my waist. I gently picked it up and started giving it to her from the back. The duo playing but we both ignored it Crystal laid flat on my stomach while I gently on her back giving it to her again. The doorbell rang again. "ohhh baby go see who it is." "After I get this last nut." I said going faster and faster the both of us collapsed on the bed smiling at one another. "Now will you go get the door?" Crystal said.

I put all my boxes in and went to open the door and as I opened the door Kevin came and stormed inside my curb.

"Kevin, don't you know how to call first before you come storming in here?"

"You just don't understand man."

"Understand what?"

"The bitch is crazy man think she's my boss I'm going end up catching a case son."

"Then why the fuck are you still with Keisha?"

"That's why I said you just don't understand man you ain't never been in love."

"Excuse me then what do you call Crystal and have?"

Man, you've known her for what three months, and already you're in love? That's what I'm talking about it ain't real. That's why I said you wouldn't understand.

Kevin was right about one thing Crystal and I did fall in love fast, but it happens. We met one another at a party Kevin and I went to around West 4th St. I knew Kristen was a sexy lady by the way she danced. I made sure I her that night after I gave her my number and told her to call she called immediately telling me to call her anytime. That's the good thing about caller ID and asked for a few dates Crystal and I became a couple we were both looking for the same thing. She wanted a man to love I respect her. I wanted a woman who could give me the same thing I could give her in return which was love. Crystal was exactly what I wanted, but according to Kevin, she wasn't what I needed. "Real talk Kevin you need to give Crystal more credit."

"Give Crystal credit for what?" Crystal said as she kissed me.

"It's nothing baby I was just explaining to Kevin how special you are to me." I said looking back at Kevin.

"And don't you forget it all boo?" She said as she kissed me goodbye and just looked at Kevin and left.

Seeing Kevin act like this was nothing new he even went and sat on the couch.

"Shemar you can't get mad at a brother for looking out for his boy."

"I never said I was mad at you. All I said was you need to give her more credit."

"Give her credit for what? I mean how well do you know Chrystal? Did you even meet a family?"

"Her families in Trinidad, And yes I know Chrystal she's on her way to her second job now."

"And do you even know where her second job is?"

"I cut Kevin, love, right there. Son, what is it you got against my lady? It's like you got something against me be a faithful Chrystal."

Look Shemar as I said before you shouldn't put all your cards in when you have one hand to play. "Kevin and I were still in our early 20s we should begin as much experience as we could, with all types of women that were willing to give it up. My father passed away when I was eight due to a heart attack so my mother and uncle raised me to be the man I am today. I have had my share of women before Crystal and I met each other.

"Look Kevin I'm not about to mess up my relationship with Crystal for a chick that's just a one-night stand. "All right all right let's at least go hang out at a club and have a few drinks."

Kevin was my boy, and we hadn't hung out in a while so I agreed. He smiled, but I wanted him to understand that accepting the relationship between Crystal and I was serious.

Coming
2017

Year of the
Gentlemen

You'll fall in love
with the members's
at
Real creation's

a novel by
Kasim Power

www.ingramcontent.com/pod-product-compliance
Lightning Source LLC
Chambersburg PA
CBHW070805050426
42452CB00011B/1895